Am I Not Still God?

Am I Not Still God?

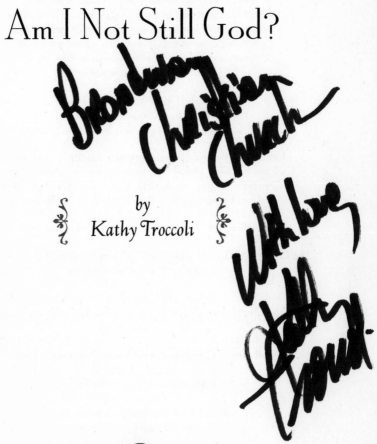

§ by §
Kathy Troccoli

W PUBLISHING GROUP™

www.wpublishinggroup.com

A Division of Thomas Nelson, Inc.
www.ThomasNelson.com

Am I Not Still God?

Published by W Publishing Group,
a Division of Thomas Nelson, Inc.,
P. O. Box 141000, Nashville, Tennessee, 37214.

Library of Congress Cataloging-in-Publication Data
Troccoli, Kathy.
Am I not still God? / by Kathy Troccoli.
p. cm.
Includes bibliographical references (p.).
ISBN 0-8499-1709-3 (hc)
ISBN 0-8499-4398-1 (tp)
1. Suffering—Religious aspects—Christianity.
2. Christian life. I. Title.
BV4909 .T76 2002
248.8'6—DC21
2001056897

Printed in the United States of America
03 04 05 06 07 PHX 9 8 7 6 5 4 3

Dedicated
to the memory of
my dear mother and father,
Josephine and Frank

Contents

ACKNOWLEDGMENTS   IX

PART 1: STORMS
Looking Around

Chapter 1
Am I Not Still God?   3

Chapter 2
Where Are You?   21

Chapter 3
Brace Yourself   43

PART 2: THE SHELTER
Looking Up

Chapter 4
Always Present   71

Chapter 5
Never without Hope   97

Chapter 6
Complete Trust   131

vii

PART 3: SAILING ON
Looking Ahead

Chapter 7
Winds of Faith 155

Chapter 8
Wounded Healer 177

Epilogue
The Mourning After 201

NOTES 205

SOURCES FOR SONGS 209

Acknowledgments

For their generous love and support, I wish to thank Dee Brestin, Matt Baugher, Mark Sweeney and W Publishing, Debbie Wickwire, Linda Montero, Todd and Peggy Schilling, my Prayer Team, Kathy Decker, and Glena Jacobs.

Part 1
Storms

❧ Looking Around ❧

Chapter 1
Am I Not Still God?

I was fourteen years old. Usually my Saturdays began with my mother cooking up a huge breakfast for my dad, my sister, and me. It was a weekly ritual to have hot rolls and eggs. Even now the aroma of fresh-brewed coffee reminds me of those special times with my family.

But this Saturday morning was different.

For the last couple of weeks my dad had been losing weight, and on this morning he had awakened with strange pains in his stomach and looked pale and gray. He couldn't stop vomiting. My mother immediately put him in the car and left for the emergency room. As she left in a panic, she told my sister and me to have breakfast next door at my aunt's house. We knew something was wrong, but we didn't know *how* wrong.

With each hour that passed, I worried more. Something was definitely not right. Every time the phone rang, my heart jumped but my spirit sank. I had an awful premonition that we were going to hear terrible news.

A storm was brewing that was going to turn my life upside down, close the door of childhood forever, and force me to begin a journey that would lead me into pondering life and death, suffering, eternity, and the heart of God.

Without Warning a Furious Squall Came Up

Finally Mom called. All I heard my aunt say was, "Oh, my God! Seventy-two hours to live?"

I thought, *Am I hearing right?* It turned out that cancer had infested Dad's colon and peritonitis was poisoning his system. He ended up living eleven more months. I look back now and think, *How could a young teenager have understood what was going on?* It was almost as if I were in some sort of weird fog. I don't think I ever acknowledged how sick my dad was. I don't think I really believed he would die. He was my dad. He was strong. He worked all the time. He never got sick. Besides . . . this was an awful intrusion into our lives. I am ashamed to say that many days of my adolescence were infused with a subtle selfishness. I watched my mom lose an incredible amount of weight as she continued to work, take care of my sister and me, and attend to all the duties of being deeply committed to a dying man. I often think about how she also managed to hide her own pain.

My dad was a printer in New York City. He was a foreman with many responsibilities. Every day Frank Troccoli needed to meet deadlines, handling numerous gigantic printing presses. His job made his hands different from those of any of my friend's fathers. No matter how much he cleaned them up, the lines in his fingertips were engraved with dark black ink. He worked hard. He worked long hours. He lived for the weekends.

I grew up in a little town called Islip Terrace, Long Island, from where my dad would take the 5:30 train every morning into the heart of New York City. He would usually come home anywhere between 6:30 and 8:30 at night. Yes, Saturday and Sunday were his days. They were also the only days I would get to spend any time with him. What I remember most about him was that he was consistently kind and good-natured. He loved people and was extremely social. There were many summers when my parents would throw big pool parties in our backyard. Lots of food. Lots of laughter. Lots of fun. My dad took so much pride in how his house and his yard looked. The majority of my time with him was spent mowing the lawn, or weeding around the bushes and fences. At the end of the day, with sweaty bodies and dirty hands, we would look around at our freshly groomed part of the world. He would have this look of contentment on his face, and I would always know that it had been a day well spent.

My dad was five-foot-eight and stocky. He always looked so strong to me. He acquired the famous "beer gut" that can work its way onto the physique of many men, but he kept shoulders and arms that were solid and athletic looking. That is why it grieved me to watch his body become slight and frail as it was ravaged by cancer.

I talk about Dad being a printer and also of my fond memories of us working together on hot Saturdays making our yard look like a paradise. It's funny, because two specific memories, pertaining to each of these things, have stayed with me, deeply etched in my heart.

As my father became more ill, it was obvious that he could not keep up with the responsibilities of his job. Just traveling to the City to work exhausted him before he even began his workday. I know it broke his heart not to be capable of doing what he loved doing. I remember a specific day when Mom took my sister and me to McDonald's. On the way home she said that we were going to visit my dad at his new job. I will never forget what I felt when I walked through the doors of what looked like an old barn. My heart experienced a strange kind of breaking. There, in the midst of lots of old wood and sawdust, was my father. He was working with one little printing press alongside an elderly man. This man owned and ran this tiny printing business in his backyard. My dad greeted us with a big smile on his face, and I realize now how humbling it must have been for him to work in conditions that were so inferior to his former position. It has spoken to me many times of his work ethic and his integrity.

I often think about what it would have been like if my father had lived. I would have loved to relate to him, not just as a little girl, but as an adult woman. I often think he would be proud of me. He absolutely gave me a love for people, and I pray I'm giving him the honor of being a woman who yearns to have the heart of God. When I first started singing, my dad would knock on my bedroom door and say,

Please sing for me. Sing for Daddy.

I would oftentimes be annoyed at the interruption or would say something like,

Not now, Dad. I don't feel like it.

He would reply like a child,

Come on. Just a little bit. Just one song.

Boy . . . do I wish I had serenaded him more. Each time my voice rises toward heaven, I hope my dad gets to hear the song.

And the Waves Swept over the Boat

It was May 24, 1974. I was in biology class. My name was called over the loudspeaker to report to the main office. All the students stared at me with a deafening silence. They knew my father had been dying. As I approached the lobby of the school, my grandfather and my aunt took my hand and led me to the car. Not a word was spoken as we drove the couple of miles home that felt like an eternity. I walked into my house to utter chaos. Family members were crying. Some were angry and saying a lot of "If only the doctors would have . . ." kinds of things. People were grabbing me and hugging me tightly, which annoyed me and stifled me more than comforted me. I needed to explode. I'm not sure about all the emotions I was feeling—of course the obvious ones—but all I can tell you is that they were piercing and I was experiencing the weight of them.

I ran outside into the backyard. Our yard was huge. It always seemed like forever to mow it all. Now the grass was high and the weeds were overtaking the beauty I once knew. My father was dead, and so was the ground I was looking at. There seemed to be thousands of dandelions around my feet. All I could do was tear into them. I ripped and I pulled. I kicked and I screamed. With every yank there seemed to be less pressure in my body, and I broke into a loud cry.

Save Me, Lord; I'm Drowning!

I know you understand, because though you may not have lost a parent when you were a child, you have experienced pain—and sometimes it has been overwhelming. I know because Jesus said this life would be full of trouble. I know because I have talked to you. God has blessed me enormously by giving me a voice, by opening doors of ministry for me, and by allowing me to meet you. Often the time I spend at my book table after a seminar is much longer than the time I have had onstage. This is my time to meet you, to pray with you, to listen to your hearts. I know storms are a part of life, and many of you tell me how the waves are sweeping over your boat. You have been calling to Jesus, pleading for His help. Some of you have stopped calling. Life has been too hard.

Just in the last few months, even in the last few days, these are some of the things I have heard:

> *A young mother of three—who is a new believer in Jesus Christ—walks into the bedroom of her youngest son, a two-and-a-half-year-old boy, only to find his body cold and still. He died inexplicably in the middle of the night.*

> *A single woman who often comes to my concerts is on vacation with her best friend in the Bahamas.*

8

She takes a long walk in the middle of a beautiful sunny day and is raped.

A handsome man—so kind and charming—struggles every day with his "thorn." His desires are not for women but for men.

A sweet couple—so eager and ready to be a mommy and daddy—have tried everything under the sun to conceive a child and her womb remains barren.

A vibrant, strong girl finishes her last treatment for breast cancer, and discovers that the cancer has just traveled into her bones.

I could fill the pages of this book—maybe even the books in an entire library—with more sad stories just like these. I know some of you could too. Every single day, life unfolds—revealing terrible tragedies along with sheer joys . . . carrying every emotion and circumstance imaginable or unimaginable. Life's slow unfolding stops for no one.

Sometimes the fists punch toward heaven, sometimes the tears flow like a gushing river, sometimes those tears are held back by a dam of anger—and sometimes, knees fall to the ground as a soul abandons everything to the One in control of it all.

How many times do you think Almighty God has heard . . .

Why is this happening?

How could You allow this?

If You were a loving God . . .

That person doesn't deserve this!

Where are You?

These questions have been ringing in God's ears from the Garden of Eden all the way into the twenty-first century. We don't understand His ways, we question His wisdom, we wrestle with our faith, and ultimately, we wonder, *Just how much can I trust God?*

Can you blame us? We are trapped in a casing of flesh and blood. Even when God came to earth in the form of man, He asked, "Why?" from the cross. We have finite minds, fickle hearts, and failing bodies. What do we know? Yet when a question of life or death comes at us—of what is fair or not fair, right or not right—we want answers.

And then in the midst of it all . . . God doesn't necessarily give us an answer, but He asks us a question. Amidst all of our anger. Amidst all of our doubts. Amidst all of our sadness and our questions. He asks a question back.

Like so many of you, my life has been filled with seasons of extreme heartache. Notice that I said "seasons"; there hasn't been one major heartbreak, there's been a series of them. When I committed my life to Christ, did He wipe away pain and make my life like a day at Disney World? Did stardust fall from the sky? Did each new day display a brilliantly colored rainbow? Were there no more problems, no more pain, and no more PMS?

Oh, if only it were so. . . .

Where Is Your Faith?

In 1991, the Lord asked me a question that pierced through the very essence of my faith and the very depths of my heart. Some of you have heard me share this at concerts and conferences through the years . . . but bear with me as I reveal for the first time to so many others the life-changing conversation that took place ten years ago between God and me.

My dear mother, Josephine, had discovered a lump in her breast in 1989. It was diagnosed as cancerous so she had a mastectomy, without any complications. At that time, no chemotherapy or radiation was advised. She did go for regular checkups and was told that all was well. I would take her to these appointments, and we would always leave with a big sigh of relief and a burden of anxiety lifted.

I remember when Mom first told me that the tumor was indeed cancerous. I had come home one afternoon to find her holding her sister's hand as they sat close together on the living-room couch. I could tell something was wrong. There was a solemn vacuum of sadness in the air that felt like most of the oxygen had been sucked out of the room. As I walked over to them, my mom looked up at me and said nervously,

Kathleen, the doctor told me that it's cancer.

She had tears in her eyes and a childlike quiver in her voice.

What did I do? How did I respond? I could kick myself when

I think about it. A couple of passionate angry words came out of my mouth as I exited the room in a fury. With each step up the stairs I pounded my feet deep into the carpet, then reached my bedroom—and slammed the door as hard as I could.

At that point it was all about me. It didn't matter that my precious mother was downstairs shaking like a frightened squirrel. It just mattered that I was disgusted—and steaming mad. Wasn't it enough that I had watched my young father waste away as cancer ate its way through his body? I couldn't comprehend that this might also happen to my mother.

It all gets a little fuzzy from here. While Mom went through the surgery with a speedy recovery, I think I felt numb. I knew people would pray. I requested some prayer and sent my own handful of "flash" prayers toward heaven. But I settled into a "coasting" season in my Christianity, and before I knew it, Mom seemed like her old self again.

Fast-forward two and a half years. My mother started complaining about stomachaches and extreme tiredness. I noticed a bit of a weight loss. She put off going to the doctor. She hated going to the doctor. She would always say things like, "It's just a bug," or "It will go away." I knew something was wrong when her skin started getting a yellow hue, and I pleaded with her to go and get checked out. When I took her to our regular physician, it was Christmas Eve day. I saw his face as he looked over her body and asked her some questions.

"Could it be hepatitis?" my mom asked sheepishly.

"Maybe," he said quietly. He told her to get some x-ray work done right after Christmas.

I went down the hallway to get a minute alone with him. "It's not hepatitis, is it, Doctor?"

I remember him taking a deep breath, avoiding my eyes—and saying, "It doesn't look good."

We went through Christmas and New Year's acting like Mom had hepatitis. "Don't touch. Don't cook. Don't clean. Keep your hands off of everything." My sister believed the deception. I had a sinking feeling in my heart the whole time. I remember looking across the room at my mother during our family's little New Year's Eve celebration. She looked much more yellow now. Peaked. Thin. I knew something was desperately wrong. With a big smile on my face I wrapped my arms around her—but behind my eyes were a million tears.

It was Valentine's Day, 1991. After a series of tests and discussions with doctors, we decided on surgery at Sloan-Kettering Hospital in New York City. Mom was to undergo an operation to see exactly what was going on inside of her. The "waiting room" was a gigantic lobby with overstuffed chairs and couches. Some people were pacing. Some people were praying. I kept glancing up at the clock and glancing toward the postop room. The hands on the clock seemed stuck. The hall remained empty. The waiting was excruciating. I couldn't sit still, I couldn't concentrate, and I couldn't keep my thoughts from racing into frightening scenarios. . . .

> *Troccoli. Kathy Troccoli. Please report to the front desk.*

A nurse didn't visit me. I got a sterile voice calling to me over a loudspeaker.

My heart felt like it was going to blast a hole through my chest as I walked over to the phone that was being handed to me.

"Yes?" I whispered.

"This is Doctor . . ." His voice seemed to fade in and out as I struggled to focus beyond the hurricane whirling in my brain.

"We have found multiple tumors throughout her liver and pancreas. There isn't much we can do."

"Well, what does this mean?" I said.

"About six months to two years—I'm very sorry."

I hung the phone up in a complete daze of disbelief. I wanted to scream—I wanted to run—I wanted to climb out of my body.

The Waters Raged

I remember being aware of a little chapel down the hall from the lobby. It's as if someone took my hand and led me in that direction. I stumbled through the doors and lay across a pew. To this day I am so thankful that not a single soul was in there. It was dark and extremely quiet. My cries echoed around the room. I held my face in my hands and felt emotion roll over me in tidal waves. Anger to sadness. Sadness to anger. "What is going on? Where the heck are You, Lord?" I had so much internal energy. Put me in the ring. I was ready for a boxing match. Tired of cancer. Sick of life. It was too hard. Way too hard . . . and . . . not fair. Definitely not fair.

I kicked and screamed . . . then fell into a ball of tears. When I caught my breath, I kicked and screamed some more . . . only to fall back down again into a helpless heap. My face was drenched and swollen. My eyes could not look up. I was exhausted in my mind and in my spirit. I lay still.

Am I not still God?

Silence.
"What?" I barely whispered out loud.

Am I not still God?

The Almighty. The Lord of heaven and earth. It was unmistakable. I knew it was His voice that was penetrating the very core of my soul.

How could I ignore Him? Something in me wanted to. There was such a war going on inside of me. A part of me wanted to go at it with Him—and then run away, behind the tallest, fattest wall I could find. But oh . . . the biggest part of me wanted to run toward Him. Run as fast as I could into the arms of the One I knew was greater than I. He was there. I knew He was waiting for an answer.

I bowed my head. I relinquished my will.

Yes, Lord. You are still God.

The Storm Subsided and All Was Calm

I often think back to that time in that little chapel at Sloan-Kettering Hospital. It was supernatural. It was life changing. Corrie ten Boom once said:

> *I can declare that the deepest darkness is outshone*
> *by the light of Jesus.*[1]

A deep darkness. A beacon of light from Jesus. He was my hope. He *is* my hope.

In the story of Jesus and the disciples, Jesus stopped the storm on the sea. In my story, He calmed the storm in my heart. How did He do it? By healing my mother? No. He did it by teaching me something about Himself. I want to talk about something that I find so interesting about God. He never ceases to amaze me or surprise me. The words of the Scriptures are ever so true:

> *For my thoughts are not your thoughts,*
> *neither are your ways my ways. . . .*
> *As the heavens are higher than the earth,*
> *so are my ways higher than your ways*
> *and my thoughts than your thoughts.*
> —ISAIAH 55:8–9

That day at the hospital, I had so many questions spinning in my head. As each one furiously swirled in, it seemed to immediately burst out of my mouth. *Why? Why?* And more *Why?*s. As all of my *whys* flung toward heaven, you would think that the God of all wisdom would hear each question—catch each question—and throw back some "good" answers. I mean, if He knows it all—why wouldn't He just tell me? And even if He didn't want to explain it all to me, you would think that He would at least speak to me in ways that were comforting and tender. Sometimes the Lord is awfully lavish with words—take a look in the Bible—and that day I could have used a . . .

Please don't be mad at Me. I really love you.

16

Or maybe something like . . .

> *I'm here. Calm down, My sweet child. Let Me hold you.*

Or I think I really would have totally melted if I'd heard Him say . . .

> *Your mother won't die. Everything will work out exactly like you want it to.*

Wouldn't that have been the ultimate? And isn't that what we would all like to hear?

I often visit my dear friends Allyson and Brent in Anderson, Indiana. They have three little boys whom I adore. Logan is six, Jordan is four, and Jared is two. One day while Allyson was out with Logan and Jared, Jordan and I decided to watch the movie *Ever After*. It's one of my all-time favorite movies and supposedly the "real" story of Cinderella. Drew Barrymore delivers an exquisite performance of this endearing character, and I must confess that I have watched this film a few zillion times. So here comes the scene where the prince arrives to rescue Cinderella out of the hands of the nasty villain. He runs to her . . . professing his undying love. She is worn and tattered, and yet her smile is beautiful and radiant as she cries with joy, filled with the knowing that she is loved and that her prince has come to take her away. . . .

I was sitting with my legs flung over the side of the living-room chair as Jordan lay on the carpet with his knees bent— one leg crossed over the other. I either cry or tear up at this same point in the movie every time I watch it, so I knew I would be doing one or the other as the lovers embraced— and Cinderella's pain turned into promise. As Jordan heard the sound of my sniffles, he turned around and looked at me. This innocent heart knew exactly what I was feeling. He asked ever so sweetly,

Do you want to live in this movie, Coli?

Yes I do, Jordy. I sure do.

We want the fairy tale. We want the happy ending. We want to have what God had originally intended for us to experience in the Garden. The dynamic speaker and author Patsy Clairmont says:

Look up fair in your concordance. It ain't there!

Getting back to God's conversation with me in the chapel, He never gave me the answer I wanted. As a matter of fact, He didn't even give me an answer. Instead, He asked me a question:

Am I not still God?

Out of the Whirlwind

Again and again in Scripture, God asks a question of the person who is suffering. Perhaps the most famous example is the closing of the Book of Job. For thirty-seven chapters Job has been asking why he has had to suffer so. Finally, after thirty-seven chapters of silence, Job hears from God:

> *Then the LORD answered Job out of the storm.*
> *He said: "Who is this that darkens my counsel*
> *with words without knowledge?*
> *Brace yourself like a man;*
> *I will question you,*
> *and you shall answer me."*
>
> —JOB 38:1–3

From the beginning of time, this has been God's pattern. God allows His beloved to face a storm, and then, out of the storm, He is the One with questions. This pattern began in the Garden. Do you remember?

Chapter 2
Where Are You?

I love the fact that God has wanted to communicate intimately with us since the beginning of creation. He has chosen His words carefully and has used them in so many different ways. With them, He has often instructed us, comforted us, rebuked us, and convicted us. I know that in my own life nothing has pierced the very core of me like the Word of God. There are times when I have been so bound in the cords of anger, and then I'll read a couple of His words and feel my heart melt like ice under hot water. I have been so broken and so heartsick, then I've read a psalm or heard a song about Him and a supernatural hope has mended my wounds.

I remember one time in particular when the Lord spoke to me directly and specifically from His Word. I had moved to Nashville, Tennessee, in 1980. I was a baby Christian, had made my first record, and had started traveling all over the United States. It was such a challenging and overwhelming time for two reasons. The first being that before I moved there I had hardly been anywhere but Long Island, New York. I had lived a pretty sheltered existence. My extended family was "my neighborhood," and "macaroni" was a staple food on Sundays. Pasta was to our family what rice is to the Japanese. There were diners, delis, and pizzerias on every corner. Most people sounded like Rocky. Big, gold chains were the norm as far as the jewelry that adorned the necks of both men and women.

The other reason is that I had definitely not been a "church girl" growing up. I considered myself a "Chreaster." I went to church on Christmas and Easter. Church was not a big deal. When you asked my friends or family where they were getting married, they would tell you the catering hall where the party was being thrown. The service was a minor part of the whole event. I remember going to Brown Bannister's wedding in Nashville. (He was the producer of my very first record.) We all retreated to the basement of the church after the service. I was sipping a drink of punch and chomping on a cookie when I looked at my watch. We had been there for about forty-five minutes. I turned to my friends and said, "When are we going to the wedding reception?" A shocked look came upon all of their faces. As if I were some ignoramus, they all said, "You *are* at the reception." You see, my cultural background is different. Italian wedding receptions in New York can go on for five hours. You have a cocktail hour, a dinner hour, a dessert hour . . . and then a couple of hours later breakfast might be served! Mind you, I am just touching the surface of my experiences in the early eighties as a transplant from the Northeast. I'll never forget a man coming up to me after I gave a concert in a little church somewhere in the South. He shook my hand and with a big smile on his face declared loudly,

> *Wow! I've neyver meyut an Eyetalian Chreeshtian befawer!*

Whew . . . I must tell you, though, that I now reside in Nashville half of my year and absolutely love the South and its people. I just wasn't prepared for all the changes and discoveries that quickly came my way.

Then there was the disillusionment with the "church" and the Christian music industry. Finding Jesus had been such a revelation for me. It was all so new. I thought I was going to meet and encounter all sorts of wonderfully godly people. I did. But they were few and far between. Don't misunderstand what I am saying . . . I want to throw myself in that arena too. I'm not so smug as to let you think I am without hypocrisy. I had and still have my own set of baggage. But I was a baby believer, and I thought every Christian would have abounding love in their hearts. I thought people who preached the gospel, *lived* the gospel. I thought there would be no malice or gossip or evil. I was devastated by what I was seeing. I thought, *Where do you go if you don't find Christ in Christians?* I now realize, and thank God, that we can always go to the Source Himself.

This Poor Woman Called and the Lord Heard Her

So in the midst of all this cultural and emotional upheaval, the Lord tenderly met me. I needed to know that He was there. I was at church one Sunday weeping silently. I sensed the Lord wanting me to read Psalm 34. What a beautiful piece of Scripture. I often return to it to remind myself of God's heart toward me. It is my absolute favorite. Picture me reading this psalm through blurry eyes. My tears fell on the pages. I'll pull out some different parts of it for you. This is how I read it to myself:

> *I will extol the* LORD *at all times;*
> *his praise will always be on my lips.*
> *My soul will boast in the* LORD;
> *let the afflicted hear and rejoice.*
> *Glorify the* LORD *with me;*
> *let us exalt his name together.*
>
> *I sought the* LORD, *and he answered me;*
> *he delivered me from all my fears.*
> *Those who look to him are radiant;*
> *their faces are never covered with shame.*
> *This poor [woman] called, and the* LORD *heard [her];*
> *he saved [her] out of all [her] troubles.*
> *The angel of the* LORD *encamps around those*
> *who fear him,*
> *and he delivers them. . . .*
>
> *Fear the* LORD, *you his saints,*
> *for those who fear him lack nothing. . . .*
>
> *Turn from evil and do good;*
> *seek peace and pursue it.*

> —PSALM 34:1–7, 9, 14

Though these words have ministered to countless believers over the ages, that Sunday morning, in the midst of all my pain, I felt that the angel of the Lord was encamping around *me*, that the Lord was tenderly speaking to *me*. I often talk about "being kissed by the King," which happens at those amazing, intimate moments when you sense God's presence in a tangible way. He was kissing away my tears, kissing away my heartache. I kept reading, hungry for more.

Oh, how I love this next part:

> *The eyes of the LORD are on the righteous*
> *and his ears are attentive to their cry. . . .*
>
> *The righteous cry out, and the LORD hears them;*
> *he delivers them from all their troubles.*
> *The LORD is close to the brokenhearted*
> *and saves those who are crushed in spirit.*
>
> *A righteous [woman] may have many troubles,*
> *but the LORD delivers [her] from them all;*
> *he protects all [her] bones,*
> *not one of them will be broken.*
>
> —PSALM 34:15, 17–20

I no sooner picked my head up when the Holy Spirit said,

> *Wait for My sign. I want you to read this to the congregation. It will bless them. It will also be a sign for you that I heard your cry.*

The Lord is Close to the Brokenhearted

About five minutes later, as worship filled the auditorium, the music leader said, "Let's read Scripture to one another." This was the sign for which God had told me to wait. I bowed my head as more tears began to flow freely down my face. I got up and stood behind the podium and read that psalm with the biggest lump in my throat. What a comfort to sense Him right by my side.

As I read the Bible, I realize that the Lord never wastes any words. Even when I have listened to Him in the silence of my own heart, I know He has carefully chosen how He has spoken to me. The other thing that is so comforting and at the same time a bit unsettling is that with His words He will always tell us the truth—and wants us to get to the truth. I think we sometimes take glances at the Word of God and oftentimes barely speak to Him because we are afraid of what we will see or hear. Self-disclosure is a very difficult thing to achieve.

His Ears Are Attentive to Their Cry

And yet the Lord continues to gently invade those places in us that we have endeavored to protect with neat little walls.

Surely you desire truth in the inner parts;
you teach me wisdom in the inmost place.

—PSALM 51:6

The Lord teaches us, not just to let us see ourselves correctly, but to help us see Him correctly. I believe that's why so many times in the Scripture He asks a question. There are so many other ways He can approach us, and yet He chooses to ask questions. These questions began at the very beginning.

It happened right there in the Garden. God had just created the waters, the skies, and the land. He created the animals, the plants, the fish, and the birds. Then He created man. He created Adam and Eve in His image. One can hardly believe this majestic display of the power of God. I have read that some scientists have said that the number of stars in the universe is equal to the number of grains of sand on all the beaches of the earth! Then, think about the complexity of our bodies . . . the way we are put together . . . our ability to think and feel and communicate. It's all so mind-boggling!

So here are Adam and Eve. These two beautiful and intricate creations of God. They are bathed in innocence, without sin, and are given anything and everything they will ever need. Then one day they decide to disobey the Lord and do exactly the one thing He asked them not to do. Isn't that just like us? We want what we want—and then we want some more. Many, many times we have a choice to obey, but we always feel like we're missing out on something. It could be sexual, material, or emotional. We end up going and getting "our fill"—then suffering some huge consequences, and running from God. Sometimes we are even blaming Him as we go further and further into the distance. What we don't realize is that the distance soon becomes a dark abyss without Him. Some of us have the soberness of heart and mind to run right back to Him. I continue to pray that all of us can learn to always make the latter choice. What havoc we wreak on our own lives when we refuse to repent!

I love the writings of Oswald Chambers. He said:

> *When once we lose sight of God, we begin to be reckless, we cast off certain restraints, we cast off praying, we cast off the vision of God in little things, and begin to act on our own initiative. If we are eating what we have out of our own hand, doing things on our own initiative without expecting God to come in, we are on a downward path, we have lost the vision.*[1]

Let's move on to see what happens next in the Book of Genesis:

> *Then the man and his wife heard the sound of the LORD God as he was walking in the garden in the cool of the day, and they hid from the LORD God among the trees of the garden. But the LORD God called to the man, "Where are you?"*
> —GENESIS 3:8–9

"Where are you?" Boy, if that wasn't a loaded question. Do you think the God who created the heavens and the earth needed to ask that question? "Wow, Adam! I'm so sorry. I made so many of these bushes. . . . I just can't seem to find you!" Absolutely not. Of course the Lord knew where Adam and Eve were.

He Desires Honesty

I have learned that the Lord is always on a pursuit to get to the heart of the matter. "Where are you?" Those three words represent so much. He was after something. He desired something. Something way beyond what He was asking. . . .

What God desired was honesty. He wanted Adam and Eve to answer Him with the truth. He desired for His children to realize where they were. Tell Him where they were. That would be their first step in realizing the state of their hearts and their desperate need for Him. What we are doing when we are honest is turning the light on in the blackness of our souls. How foolish to hold back the truth from Almighty God! He already sees our slate. Who are we kidding?

When He asked me that powerful question in the chapel at the hospital, I was certainly sure He knew the answer. He didn't need me to tell Him if He was God or not. "Please, Kathy. Please tell Me I'm God. I'll feel much more secure and confident about Myself." I don't think so. The Lord wanted to get to the very core of my faith. Did I believe Him? Had He abandoned me? Was Jesus God just in times of joy? I knew He wanted me to answer that question so that I would choose where I would live and how I would live. On which side of the mountain would I pitch my tent?

I was at a women's conference recently where verses from Deuteronomy 30 were displayed on a big screen. I knew immediately that I should include them in this book. God (through Moses) specifically and directly addressed the Jews:

This day I call heaven and earth as witnesses against you that I have set before you life and death, blessings and curses. Now choose life, so that you and your children may live and that you may love the LORD your God, listen to his voice, and hold fast to him.

— VERSES 19–20

Choosing life. Holding fast to Him. It is our decision. God will never force Himself and His will on anyone. He will let us decide. And speaking of holding fast, I could have definitely held fast to the things I was feeling that day the doctor gave me the heart-wrenching news about my mother.

I'm sick of cancer.

I am done fighting my way through this life. It's too hard.

Don't ask one more thing of me, Lord.

What's the point in living?

Those thoughts swirled through my brain countless times. But it is when I said, "Yes, Lord" that a major stake was put in the ground. My tent was pitched in God's camp. It was the beginning of my being protected from bitterness. Its ugliness not only would have devastated my soul, but it would have spilled over onto my mother, my sister, my friends, and my family.

What we choose has very deep consequences. Our choice will affect not only our well-being but the well-being of others. Be honest. Be honest with God and be honest with yourself. Choosing Him is the doorway into a life filled with much more peace. It will open you up to hear, see, and experience the wonders of relationship with the Maker of your soul. It will draw you nearer to the heart of God. You will continually discover that there's no place like Him.

He Desires Communication

In the July 1991 issue of *Home Life* magazine, one hundred lawyers were asked the question "What is the major cause of divorce in American marriages?" All one hundred lawyers agreed that a breakdown in marital communication was the leading cause of divorce. Every meaningful relationship requires significant communication. We get tired. We get lazy. We get selfish in our own pursuits of what we wish to enjoy in life.

Ever since the Garden, the Lord has yearned to communicate with us. Not just on a church pew or at some retreat in the mountains, but *every single day*. In the miraculous and in the mundane. He wants communication to be continual. There is a cartoon strip in most national papers depicting the life of Leroy Lockhorn and his wife. Leroy's response to his wife one day as she was begging for communication was,

Sure we can talk; just don't block the TV.

I have to chuckle because I can't tell you how many times

I do that in my relationship with Jesus. He longs for me to talk with Him and I end up trying to communicate over the radios and stereos . . . over the phones ringing and the appointments. I leave Him waiting in the living room while I scurry about my life attending to what I think are the issues at hand. How silly to keep God on hold. We only end up keeping ourselves from the treasures of heaven. We end up keeping ourselves from the very things our hearts need to thrive. Instead, we just survive.

> *The LORD confides in those who fear him.*
> —PSALM 25:14

What else do we really need to know in this life if we can know the very heart of God? Not only has He ordained us to communicate with Him intimately, but He truly desires to reveal His heart and His will to us. We journey through this mortal life as if we have a "seasonal" relationship with God. "I felt close to Him last summer, but I'm feeling real far away from Him this spring." We go in and out like the tide. Today I believe Him, but tomorrow I may not. Who has left? Not God. He always stays. That's what I love about Him. Why do we easily forget about the gift we have in Jesus? A true confidant. A safe keeper of our secrets. A lover of our souls. There is an abundance of eternal treasure waiting to be discovered. There will always be mystery to God until we see Him face to face—but there is so much we could experience here and now. He longs to give us His jewels. Whether they are coming out of His mouth or displayed in the fabric of our lives, God Almighty wants to lavish us with all that He is. He always wants to let us know He loves us. And He will always find a way.

I have been so blessed to participate in the Women of Faith conferences around the country. I have been asked to be the speaker at some of them and the singer at others. It has been an amazing opportunity. To be center stage in front of thousands upon thousands of women has been a surreal experience for me. It's as if I've been invited to go on a ride at an amusement park. I step offstage and feel such exhilaration. To know it is all being used to pour God's life into the hearts of all those women is so humbling. I never take it for granted.

I've come to love all the speakers. They have embraced me, and just hearing them has challenged me to be a better speaker. I have to be honest and tell you that I had many days of feeling a bit intimidated. Especially at the beginning. When I walked into the green room, it was as if I were the new girl in high school who was sitting at the table of girls who had been friends since kindergarten. It's not that the women were "cool" to me; it's just that I was in awe of their closeness and their gifts. They are also hysterical. I am often doubled over with laughter as they tell their tales.

Thelma Wells has a heart of love. It just oozes out of her. Luci Swindoll is brilliant. She is well-read and well-traveled. Her deep voice can send a shiver up my spine. Patsy Clairmont is a gentle soul and the consummate speaker. My mouth hangs open every time I hear her. Marilyn Meberg is so witty and wise. I just love being around her. Barbara Johnson is a friend of God. A holy woman. What a witness of His life. And Sheila Walsh. She is so classy and eloquent and creative. My New York accent can either endear people or turn them off.

It's as if people are expecting me to say, "Accept Jesus or I'll break your face!" But this is not so for Sheila. Her Scottish accent always makes you feel like all will be well in the world. It's like when I watch *Touched by an Angel*.

Whether it's Roma Downey or Sheila Walsh, they can say anything and you will feel like you are sitting in God's lap. Imagine their lovely lilt as you read this:

> *Remember that time you tripped in the mud? It was pouring down rain and you were late for work. Your new suit was torn and pasted with dirt. Your stockings were ripped and your knees were bruised. A car passed by and drenched you some more as you tried to get up. But all that time God was there. He was loving you.*

You know what I mean about those Scottish accents? It sounds crazy but it's true. Anyway, I have deep admiration for all of those women.

My birthday happened to fall on a weekend when I was singing at a Women of Faith event in Washington, D.C. My friend Ellie lives there, so she came to the event. I am always extremely exhausted after these conferences. It is important to me to look as many women in the eye as I can and truly hear their stories. So when it reaches Saturday night, I just want to have a bite to eat and go to bed. Ellie told me that Patsy wanted me to come up to her room:

> *Patsy told me that she has a word for you.*

A word for me? Oh, man, Ellie. I'm going on vacation. I can't handle a word.

Kath. Stop it. You can't disappoint Patsy. She will be hurt.

OK . . . OK. I'll go.

We got out of the elevator and went searching for Patsy's room. I knocked on the door, and as it opened there was a loud "Surprise!" Ellie had arranged for this get-together weeks beforehand. It wasn't Patsy's room; it was a suite. And it was filled with all the speakers and some wonderful people associated with the conference. Everyone was hanging out on the chairs and on the floor. There were a couple of waiters there, serving the most exquisite of desserts. I *was* surprised.

After we all chatted a while, everyone went around the room speaking "words of life" over me. They participated in telling me how they felt about me and what they saw in me. I was so teary and overwhelmed. It was as if the Lord had arranged this night to reassure me of His love. To remind me of His faithfulness. To once again tell me that I was His and that my life was in His hands. And who would have thought that these words of reassurance would be spoken to me by these precious women?

We all need that kind of interaction. In fact, I encourage you to participate in that kind of dialogue with your friends and family. Whether it's at a birthday or a dinner, you will be amazed at how God can pour His encouragement and life over one's soul. Speaking words of life over someone will always be a warm rain falling upon a parched heart. Which one of us doesn't need it? Oh, what jewels the Lord longs to crown us with.

Continue to talk to Him. Talk to Jesus. Some of you are ignoring Him. Some of you feel like you need to explain everything to Him so He will "get it." Jesus doesn't need an abundance of words. He doesn't need a dissertation about your life. He just wants your attention. He wants your heart. Feel far away from Him? Move closer. Feel close? Move closer still.

He Desires Repentance

One of the cornerstones in the foundation of the Christian life is repentance. To live in a place where we continually clean out our pipes, so to speak, and let the pure river of Jesus Christ flow freely within us. Sin stops us up. It never fails. Pride and arrogance are toxic pollutants and will certainly clog the portals of our consciences. The stoppage may happen subtly and slowly or blatantly and immediately, but it will most certainly affect how we respond to God and others.

The Scriptures tell us in Genesis 3:10 that Adam hid. Adam hid! So many of us have read that passage dozens of times, but it is still so revelatory every time we read it— mostly because of the penetrating "Holy Spirit spotlight" that illuminates the darkness of our souls. Personally I must confess that I tend to get embarrassed in front of myself! Why? Because of the obvious truth. Because Adam is me. He's me. I have a tendency to run and hide. As much as I can pride myself on being "open" and "vulnerable," I want to run to the closest bush just like the next guy. Our sin makes us afraid to show ourselves. Although I could give you many examples from my own life, one in particular comes to mind. It's fairly "innocent" but has oftentimes been a reminder to me of my "hiding" and God "finding" me. It happened in the third grade. I thank God for my teacher Miss Moore. She "found me out" and offered a sweet grace. . . .

My class was learning how to use the library. In order for us to remember some of the basics, Miss Moore required us to write a book report using tools from the library. For some reason I was completely petrified of the library. It felt like a doctor's office to me. The silence intimidated me. The rows of books overwhelmed me. It even smelled "smart."

We were left in the library one afternoon to do our book reports. Each of us was given a topic. The topic that was assigned to me was citrus fruits. I had no idea what citrus fruits were. I thought to myself,

> *Maybe she gave me an easy one. It can't be that hard. Fruit. I eat fruit. I love bananas and I even like strawberry ice cream sometimes.*

I remember walking through the door of the library and feeling nauseous. A cold chill went up and down my spine. Being there felt as if someone had left me in an operating room and told me to perform brain surgery. I fumbled around through the index boxes and then roamed the aisles. I thought that if I looked like I knew what I was doing then I would fit in with the rest of my class. I grabbed a handful of books (none of which had anything to do with citrus fruits) and sat down at the long, wooden table. I surrounded myself with open books and took out my pen and paper. I wrote and I wrote. I wrote with very large letters so that I could get several pages out of my "knowledge" of citrus fruits. It went something like this:

Citrus fruits are really good. They taste so good. As a matter of fact you can grow citrus fruits in your backyard if you want to. As long as you have sun and water you can grow citrus fruits. . . .

I cringe even now as I recall this. Yes—I went on and on. I stopped writing when I thought there were enough words or enough pages. I put the books away and handed in my report. Walking out of the library was like coming up for air after you've tried to hold your breath under water.

A couple of days later, Miss Moore called me up to her desk. The other kids had been let out for recess, but she told me to stay behind. When I got close enough to her, she picked me up and put me on her lap. There in front of us was the reminder of my torture in the library. My big-lettered, lots of pages . . . book report on citrus fruits.

"Kathleen," Miss Moore said with a curious sigh. "Did you write this report?"

"Yes," I answered.

"Did you go to the library?"

"Yes," I said.

"Did you get this information out of the library books?"

"Yeeesss . . . Noooo . . ." I began to sob in her arms.

"Why did you do this?" she asked tenderly.

"I was scared. I hate the library," I said, wiping my nose on my sleeve.

She tended to my wounds of embarrassment and told me she would walk me through it herself. She assured me that everything would be all right.

We want to run. We want to hide. Although this is a small story from a little girl's life, it exemplifies how fear can control us. Then shame and guilt soon follow. We may be affected emotionally or physically, but we will most definitely be affected spiritually.

Psalm 90:8 says:

> You have set our iniquities before you,
> our secret sins in the light of your presence.

So what ends up happening is that God sees it all from the very moment we betray His trust, and with every moment that passes by without confession, a brick is laid. Tragically, there are times when we are violated by the betrayal of others. Before we know it a fortress is built around our souls and we shut ourselves off from the precious voice of the Holy Spirit and His touch upon our lives. "Don't come in!" we'll yell from inside the wall. The problem is that we've built the wall in the first place. Then we hang warning signs over the wall to assure that others won't cross over. If you have ever been inside the wall, you are probably familiar with the warning signs. See if any of these sound familiar according to your state of heart (I'll just refresh your memory a bit):

> For the angry it's—
> **D.B.M.**—don't bug me.

For the abused it's—
 K.Y.D.—keep your distance.

For the arrogant it's—
 I.D.I.M.W.—I'll do it my way.

For the stubborn it's—
 I.D.W.T.—I don't want to.

For the coward it's—
 I.S.—I'm scared.

The list goes on and on according to what frame of mind you were in when you built the wall.

The problem is that God doesn't play this game. Sure, He wants to get close to you—that is His passion—but He will not play. And you'll find that the only people who get inside the wall are the ones who hang the same warning signs over their "hideaways." Being inside your wall becomes a "safe" community for them. Like-minded people hiding behind the wall. No confrontations. No challenges. Sometimes your conversations inside the wall can even turn into murmurings against those outside the wall. You'll judge the closed-mindedness of people; you'll mock their dogmas and legalisms, when in fact you have created your own dogmatic belief systems behind the wall. It all becomes a sad state of affairs. How quickly the heart becomes occupied with thick, deceptive black clouds without the penetration of the light of the absolute truths of God.

Want to see your walls tumble down and the Holy Spirit rush in? Just confess your sin. It's about honesty. It's about communication. It's about repentance. Repentance is the dynamite that God uses to break down our barriers to Him. No matter how long you've lived inside your walls and no matter how high you've piled brick upon brick, a supernatural explosion will always occur. The most glorious part is that beyond all the rubble you will see the face of God. What a beautiful sight to behold! After you've lived in and with the lies and the darkness, the face of Jesus is a sight for sore eyes.

I must tell you a little secret about myself. In all my years of growing in my relationship with Jesus, the part of Him that has caused me to turn the quickest and the most is His love and His consistent mercy. I'm not saying that a little threat of fire and brimstone hasn't affected my choices. But I can tell you that His kindness has led me to repentance (see Romans 2:4). That truth alone has caused me to fall to my knees thousands of times. That is where I have heard the sound of my greatest weeping.

Continue to realize that He desires your closeness. It hurts Him when you stay away. That is why this verse in Psalm 51 is so powerful to me:

> *The sacrifices of God are a broken spirit;*
> *a broken and contrite heart,*
> *O God, you will not despise.*
>
> —VERSE 17

God desires honesty, communication, and repentance. When we *live* in that attitude toward Him, He will throw open the windows of heaven.

I want to tell you a story of a wonderful man who the Lord

brought into my life and who has learned these lessons well. I call him my "sweet Toddy," but he really is a contemporary Job, a man who faced storms of hurricane strength—and not just a single gale, but one after another after another. And just when he was going down for the last time, the Lord delivered him from them all.

Chapter 3
Brace Yourself

In the last several years of traveling, I have hired many different road managers. Simply put, a road manager is a person who takes care of everything concerning life on the road. He will take care of flights, hotels, and all the various accommodations needed to make everything flow easily and professionally. A road manager will talk to everyone—from the travel agent to the local church person handling an event. I have hired many. Some were good and some were bad, but all this is to say that I was recently at a point of feeling frustrated with not finding the person who was right for me.

There is so much involved in finding the right person. Not only does he need to be skilled in handling all the details of the road, but he must also be competent at running a sound system. Some people who are good at handling things on the road are not good at sound. Also, this person and I spend an enormous amount of time together. It's like a good friendship or partnership—for it to work the communication has to be solid.

Before I hired my current road manager, I was starting to feel like finding this person was such a long shot because of all the things I had gone through in the past. I was a little gun shy. My overall manager, Matt (a wonderful man who advises me with godly wisdom), and I began to pray that the Lord would send me the right man.

I first met Todd Schilling a year ago. Matt had arranged for us to meet at a popular breakfast place in Nashville. Todd was already sitting down as I rushed through the doors a little late. He has a sweet baby face and a pleasant smile, and I immediately felt comfortable with him. He was so professional. He was wearing a sports jacket and looked so well-groomed and "crisp." I, on the other hand, had on my running shorts (don't be impressed—I don't run), ball cap, and sneakers. We got acquainted and decided to give it a try.

It didn't take me long to realize the gift God was placing in my hands. Todd is an amazing sound man, understanding how to capture my voice on a microphone. He is also a great road manager. He knows exactly how to speak to people, and he takes care of me as if I were his sister. He loves Jesus and is devoted to his wife, Peggy, and their children.

The thing that affects me most about Todd is what happens to him when I am singing or speaking, when I am sharing a story or praying over people. I'll always take a peek at him at the soundboard. Sometimes his hands are raised in praise, sometimes his head is bowed in deep prayer, and sometimes he is weeping along with the others at the altar or in their seats. His heart is sensitive and tender. God knew I needed him, especially at this point in my life. What he is "about" is not just being a good guy. What has made Todd the way he is has been his suffering. I call him a "miracle boy."

Do you remember the story of Job? In many ways, Todd is a contemporary Job. I have to tell you, Job is not the book I would pick to study—sort of like going to the dentist . . . I'd just as soon skip it—but I know it's good for me, and essential to my health. So, stay with me, because understanding some of the messages conveyed in the Book of Job will help you as it has helped me with the inevitable suffering of life. And Todd's story will breathe life into this ancient story of Job.

All Is Well

When you hear the word *blameless*, it is easy to think *perfect*, but that's not what it means in the Bible. It doesn't mean a person is perfect, but that the desire of his heart is to please God. That's what the Bible says about Job. He loved God so much. He had a big family—ten kids who were grown but loved to spend time together. I picture these family gatherings sort of like a Hallmark card commercial or a Folger's ad. I've been known to have the tears start to flow as soon as the music starts and the coffee's brewed. I'm a sucker for wanting to get that warm fuzzy feeling in my heart. Just call me the "sap queen." This Old Testament family really cares about each other—lots of love, lots of thoughtful acts, Grandma Job and Grandpa Job smiling, little kids running around, lots of good food, and, most important, an overwhelming gratitude to God.

In the same way, there was a time when Todd and Peggy's life together seemed almost idyllic. Peggy describes their time of getting to know each other as a fairy-tale romance. Todd was the man of her dreams: committed to the Lord and committed to her. He constantly surprised her with what every woman wants. On any given day he would give flowers, cards, and little gifts. They were enjoying their health, their marriage, and their ministry together. They sang together at different churches. Life was sweet. Life was good.

But none of us really knows what is around the corner. One day all is well, and the next day, the bottom drops out.

Have You Considered My Servant Job?

Jill Briscoe says she's never really liked that verse, because if God could say that to Satan about Job, He could say,

Have you considered my servant Jill?

None of us wants to insert *our* name in that verse—but we all must be open to the fact that if God chooses to insert our name, He will have His way.

Satan was absolutely convinced that the only reason Job trusted God was because God had blessed him so. Job was a rich man, with a big, healthy, happy family. Here was Satan's challenge:

> *Does Job fear God for nothing? . . . Have you not put a hedge around him and his household and everything he has? You have blessed the work of his hands, so that his flocks and herds are spread throughout the land. But stretch out your hand and strike everything he has, and he will surely curse you to your face.*
>
> —JOB 1:9–11

So there you have it. God took the challenge, as Job's whole world was about to change. It may sound to you at this point like it was a game to the Lord, but God always has our best in mind. A pastor once said, "He never wounds us except to heal us." Four messengers came to Job, each with worse news than the last. This was the shocking news they brought:

> *An army came in, stole Job's oxen and donkeys, and murdered his servants.*
>
> *Fire from God burned up Job's sheep and more servants.*
>
> *Three more armies stole his camels and murdered even more servants.*
>
> *A violent wind caused the house where Job's ten children were dining to collapse—killing all of them!*

How did Job respond? In ways I only hope I would if I faced the same devastation. He fell to the ground in worship. He trusted God. He did not sin by charging the Almighty with wrongdoing.

Have You Considered My Servant Todd?

The story I am about to share with you transpired during a two-year period. This story is just astonishing. Quite frankly, it can almost seem inconceivable. I still marvel at the twists and turns of life, accompanied by the sovereign hand of God, when I hear Todd share about his unbelievable journey. . . .

It all started when his wife, Peggy, was hit by a drunk driver. This accident left her with her neck broken in three places. While Todd was visiting his wife at the hospital, he did not know that upon leaving, something would happen to him that would affect his life forever. He was on his motorcycle coming out of the parking garage, waiting for the exit gate to allow him to leave. What he couldn't see, because he had his helmet on, was the steel gate descending onto his head. He knew something drastic had happened, but his body went into shock and he kicked into "autopilot" and drove back to work in a daze.

When Todd arrived at work (he was a physical therapist), he tried to take his helmet off. He immediately knew something was seriously wrong. He felt as if he were removing his whole head along with his helmet. He was rushed to the hospital, where he found out that his neck was fractured in two places, his wrists were broken, his jaw was broken, and his lower back was fractured in three places.

Meanwhile, when Peggy underwent surgery, an anesthesiologist intubated her incorrectly and severely damaged her left vocal cord. As a result, Peggy speaks very softly with a bit of a rasp, and the quality of her singing voice has been permanently damaged.

A couple of months later, Todd and Peggy buried their second-born child, a newborn son.

How did Todd and Peggy respond? They clung to God. Like Job, they continued to worship Him, and they experienced the peace of God in the midst of all of their pain. Even as they stood in the hospital room after their baby died, cradling his tiny, lifeless body and saying good-bye with drenched faces—they trusted God. Peggy said,

> *We knew the Lord would keep His hand on us. He had helped us before, and we knew He would help us again. It was like a boxing match. We were knocked down, but we would get up. We were determined to win. We put Scriptures around the house to encourage us, taping them on the mirror, the refrigerator, wherever. We wanted to remind ourselves of the promises of God.*

Job too continued to cling to the promises of God, even when his suffering continued to increase as God allowed Satan to strike his flesh and cover him with painful sores.

For Todd and Peggy, the suffering continued to increase as well. Todd developed a rare eye disease called kerato-conus. He needed a cornea transplant in his left eye. After he had the surgery, Todd immediately flew to Montana to attend the funeral of his beloved grandfather. While he was there, his eye rejected the cornea, and he had to fly back to Indiana to undergo emergency surgery. The next day it was revealed to him that the doctors had given him an infected cornea. He had to get injections in his left eye every other day for a two-month period to try to save his sight in that eye.

During this time Todd and Peggy's house was broken into and ransacked. Most everything they had of value was stolen.

Todd underwent surgery at the University of Indiana Medical Center to repair the damage that had been done to his lower back. The doctors placed nuts, screws, rods, and bolts inside his body. I hold my breath every time Todd walks through the metal detectors at the airport security checkpoints. We never know if he'll set off the scanners.

Because of all the damage done to Todd's body from the accident, he contracted a rare disease called Reflex Sympathetic Dystrophy (RSD). This particular disease is extremely devastating. The prognosis for the disease is generally to go insane or to kill oneself—the pain is that severe and debilitating. What transpires in the body is that the pain signal is somehow transferred from the site of injury to the autonomic nervous system. The autonomic nervous system is not meant to deal with pain, so it begins to shut down. In Todd's case, the RSD began to kill the nerves and blood vessels from his feet up. He became progressively weaker. The doctors attached morphine pumps to his now "blue-jean-colored" legs. He was taking an enormous amount of pain medication just to get through a day.

The disease progressed rapidly. While Todd was at one of his weekly checkups, his doctor told him to sit down because he was about to deliver some intensely bad news. How odd it was for Todd to hear this, as if good news had been pouring in the last several months of his life. He was told that his legs would have to be amputated. As if that weren't tragic-enough news to hear, the doctor also told him that the amputation would save his life, but not take away any pain. Todd's response was immediate:

There's no way I can make that choice. I just can't

*do it. I don't know what you believe, Doctor, but
I believe that God can heal me.*

The physician responded somberly,

*I sure hope so, Todd, because that's the only hope
you've got. If you are going to do anything with
your family, do it now, and we will discuss this on
your next visit.*

When Todd got home, he didn't tell Peggy, who was pregnant again, any of the conversation that had transpired between him and his doctor. He suggested that they take a trip to Florida. Peggy's mother and father were there, and Todd thought the trip would relieve the tortuous stress they both had been living under. They were able to leave their three-year-old son, Cameron, with Todd's mother.

When Todd tells this next part of the story, you might even think I'm making up a script for an ultratragic documentary.

But it really happened.

The day they arrived in Florida, the engine blew in the van they had rented. A couple of days later, Todd and Peggy were driving home from the beach when a fully loaded semi rear-ended them at a four-way stop. This accident immediately threw Peggy into premature labor and broke Todd's jaw and both wrists. They were taken to a hospital and treated as best they could be, but they were advised to get home as soon as possible. You can imagine that any ounce of hope that was left between them was rapidly waning. Was anything ever going to be normal again?

A Devastated Man Needs
the Devotion of His Friends

When Jesus was suffering in the Garden of Gethsemane, He pleaded with His three closest friends to stay awake and to pray for Him. They totally let Him down, and it grieved Him so much. And then, another one of His friends betrayed Him with a kiss.

Job's friends came and sat with him for seven days. They saw that his suffering was great. In the same way, at first, Todd and Peggy's friends were incredibly sensitive to their suffering. But as time went on, their approach to them changed some. Like Job's friends, they began to want to know the reason for the Schillings' suffering. One pastor came to Peggy when she was in the hospital and questioned her about the "sin in their lives."

The other response that tended to increase their suffering was the tendency to make light of the situation. Job's experience was similar:

> I have become a laughingstock to my friends.
> —JOB 12:4

Peggy said, "After a while, our friends at church began to see our situation as a joke and make light of it. Maybe that was their way of dealing with it—but it certainly wasn't funny to us. We really needed them. This was the church I had grown up in, and it was so painful to hear them say these things."

You better not get in a car with Peggy and Todd!

Don't walk too close to the Schillings—it might be catching.

Oh great, something else happened to Peggy and Todd.

"What was a tragedy to us was a comedy to them."
Job says:

> *A despairing man should have the devotion of his friends.*
>
> —JOB 6:14

I heard this statement recently:

Prosperity makes friends; adversity tries them.

Who is without adversity? It is a part of life. But we were made for relationship. We were created to love God and to love each other. It is a gift to be able to love unconditionally. It is a selfless mind-set to think of others above yourself. It is "Jesus" to hold someone's hand and not let go when the storm seems to be raging around them with no end in sight. We want that kind of devotion in the midst of trouble, so we should be very aware of being at the front of the line when others need it. It takes staying close to the heart of God. We have nothing to give and no motivation to give it if we try to muster it up within ourselves. We could think of it this way: We should let God keep filling our paper towel dispenser. Then people can tear off as many as they need, and we can be totally free to give and be available because what is being given is not from us, but from God.

But Job's friends stood "far off" and condemned him. Likewise, some of Todd and Peggy's friends began to question them.

> *Peggy, are you sure there isn't something you are hiding from God?*

> *Todd, maybe there's something in your past you need to deal with.*

Peggy said, "The crazy part about all of our accidents is that none of them was our fault. That's not to say that we were without sin. But to have our friends question us intensified our grief."

Todd and Peggy began to withdraw from their friends. At a time when they needed the comfort, the prayers, and the strength of the body of Christ, they felt abandoned.

The Dialogue

There is a lot of talk in the Book of Job. Talk, talk, and more talking by the friends. The problem with all of this jabbering is that most of it is empty. Pat answers. Accusations. Condemnation. Mike Mason, in *The Gospel According to Job*, writes:

> *Probably the characteristic sin of evangelicals is this bull-in-a-china-shop approach to the consciences of other people. How often have we met*

*buttonholers like Zophar [one of Job's friends] in
the church foyer?*[1]

Job's friends thought they had all the answers. But they
didn't. As a matter of fact, we often see well-meaning people
trying to defend God, as if He needs a defense. I think the
reason why they do that is because it makes them feel better
about their own faith. If they have a defense for God, they
can explain away things in their own lives. How often God is
misrepresented. How often we want to remold Him into an
image that our hearts and minds can understand and feel
comfortable with. God revealed, at the end of the Book, the
shallowness and the ignorance of Job's friends, as He said:

> *I am angry with you . . . because you have not
> spoken of me what is right, as my servant Job has.
> So now take seven bulls and seven rams and go to
> my servant Job and sacrifice a burnt offering for
> yourselves. My servant Job will pray for you, and
> I will accept his prayer and not deal with you
> according to your folly. You have not spoken of me
> what is right, as my servant Job has.*
>
> —JOB 42:7–8

In the whole long Book of Job, it is never stated that his
friends prayed. It is constantly Job who kept crying out to God.
He constantly kept communication open with God. Isn't that
the mark of someone who has a deep relationship with the Lord?
He may not understand, but he keeps dialoguing with God.

Todd cried out to God:

*Whatever You are trying to teach me, I promise I'll
learn. Why do we have to keep going through this?
I promise You—I'll learn, I'll learn!*

David cried out to God. You can't read the Book of
Psalms without hearing his pleas. He said:

> *In the morning I lay my requests before you
> and wait in expectation.*
>
> —PSALM 5:3

And Job cried out with questions. He pleaded with God
to answer him. In anguished prayer Job stated his case, with
what I believe could have been a wrenching scream:

> *Let the Almighty answer me!*
>
> —JOB 31:35

For thirty-seven chapters God was silent. And then, out
of this horrific storm, God answered. Well, there it is again.
He questioned. It is one of the most amazing passages in
Scripture, and if you've often gotten bogged down in the
empty talk of Job's friends in the first thirty-seven chapters,
like I have, you really need to pay attention to the last five,
because that's when God speaks. God told Job:

> *Brace yourself like a man;
> I will question you,
> and you shall answer me.*
>
> —JOB 38:3

Brace Yourself

Here are a few of those million-dollar questions:

> *Where were you when I laid the earth's foundation?*

> *Have you ever given orders to the morning, or shown the dawn its place?*

> *Have the gates of death been shown to you?*

> *Can you bring forth the constellations in their seasons?*

And we are told that Job responded with humility even in the midst of all the confusion and unknowing. I can so relate to this because of my experience with God in the hospital chapel. What can you do other than fall to your knees when Almighty God speaks to you? This is what Job said:

> *I am unworthy—how can I reply to you?*
> *I put my hand over my mouth.*
> —JOB 40:4

Let's go back to Todd. His story has a similar ending. There was one significant difference in Todd's life. When things got intense for Job, his wife told him:

> *Curse God and die!*
> —JOB 2:9

When things got unbearable for Todd, Peggy managed to turn one more time toward the Lord. The night they were in the accident in Florida, she locked herself in a bathroom, feeling so weary and hopeless. She mustered up the strength to cry out to God. Not only was Todd at his end, but Peggy was also worn out by the pain and suffering they both had been going through for so long. As she hung her head and sobbed, all she heard God say in the midst of her tears was that He wanted her to praise Him.

You're kidding, right, Lord?

But somehow, and I know this because I have been there, when you know that Almighty God is speaking, you *must* hear and obey. She recalled the words to a praise song that reminded her that God would work through her if she praised Him, that God would inhabit her praise. She then began to whisper,

Praise the Lord. Praise the Lord.

She left that precious time with God with a quiet expectancy that His eye was on them and His hands were holding them. A sweet flame of hope began to flicker in her heart.

Though He Slay Me, Yet Will I Hope in Him

In Job's story, Satan was convinced that when all the blessings were removed from Job's life, Job would no longer be faithful to God. It must have been a bit discouraging to Satan to see

58

Job continue to praise God, just as it must have discouraged him to hear Peggy singing God's praises. Job passed the test earlier in the book, when he made his famous statement:

> *Though he slay me, yet will I hope in him.*
>
> —JOB 13:15

Mike Mason writes:

> *With these words, God has just won His wager with Satan. . . . Remember the devil's initial taunt, "Does Job fear God for nothing?" [Job 1:9]. Without at all realizing what he is doing, Job now delivers a direct answer to that taunt, and his answer is a resounding yes! YES!—Job's trust in God is unconditional. YES!—there is such a thing as faith that carries absolutely no ulterior motive—in other words, there is such a thing as love! And YES!—Job possesses this entirely disinterested faith and love towards God. Even if God Himself should strike him dead, Job declares, he will not cease to trust Him.*[2]

Isn't that the truth? A lot of people will tell Christians that the only reason Christians believe is because they need a "crutch," or because they are scared not to believe. Those people often see belief as weakness. I can tell you what I have observed. Most people will worship something. People were created to worship. So if you are not worshiping God, you will worship something else. I'd rather have my "weakness" be loving Jesus Christ than living a life on my own strength.

That will fail in a second. Some people also can't imagine that a love relationship is actually possible with an invisible God. They can't imagine intimacy with the Almighty. The only justification they can give for religion is that there is a "payoff." That's what Satan meant when he said, "Does Job fear God for nothing?" *The Living Bible* paraphrases Satan's response to God's mention of Job's faithfulness as: "Why shouldn't he, when you pay him so well?"

In *The Bible Jesus Read*, Philip Yancey writes that Satan implies:

> *God is not worthy of love in himself, that people follow God only because they get something out of it or are "bribed" to do so. In Satan's view, God resembles a politician who can win only by rigging the election, or a mafioso with a "kept woman" and not a devoted wife. People love God, said one priest, "the way a peasant loves his cow, for the butter and cheese it produces."*[3]

God knew something that Satan couldn't, because God could see Job's heart. He knew that Job loved Him, not because of the blessings, but because he was genuinely devoted to Him. Job wasn't living in a blameless way to get what he could from God, he was in love with God.

Yes, Job began to doubt and question why Someone he loved so much would do this to him. That is only human. God knew how much Job could take, and at the point when he was going under, God answered Job in the midst of his storm and revealed His power to him. And Job responded

just as God believed he would. God knows our hearts, inside
and out. He reminded Job with Whom he was contending—
and that's all it took. Job covered his mouth and said:

> *My ears had heard of you*
> *but now my eyes have seen you.*
> *Therefore I despise myself*
> *and repent in dust and ashes.*
> —JOB 42:5–6

God Blessed the Second Part of Job's Life More Than the First

Following Job's response of total trust, we are told, God rebuked
Job's friends and then blessed the second part of his life more
than the first. He gave him twice as much as he had before.

Let's return to Todd. Remember, we left Todd and Peggy
in Florida, where they had been rear-ended by a semi. Peggy
had experienced a supernatural visit from God, and Todd was
still losing hope by the day.

As they were getting ready to go home, Todd's father-in-
law suggested they attend a crusade that was going on in that
city. Todd wanted to be open to the idea, but he was so totally
depleted—physically, spiritually, and emotionally. He told
his family boldly,

> *If this is some hyper-spiritual, magic circus, I don't*
> *want any part of it. Besides that, a 747 might have*
> *to make an emergency landing on my head.*

Needless to say, he went. It was three hours before the crusade began when they arrived at the arena. At this point in time, Todd had digressed so much that he was walking like a crippled man. All the physically impaired people had to arrive early and were escorted to the lower level of the arena. Todd bowed his weary head and began to talk to God.

> *I don't think I can take it another day, Lord. I can't leave here the same way I came. I would rather swallow a bullet. I can't live another day like this.*

At that moment he looked up and witnessed a little old lady walking up and down the aisles praying over people. She caught his eye from a great distance away. She began to move toward him, her finger boldly pointing in his direction. As she got closer, she looked at him intensely and said,

> *Sweetheart, I don't know what your need is, but God told me that He is going to heal you.*

Todd responded almost sarcastically,

> *Well bring it on, sweetheart. I need all you got.*

She began to pray the most simple prayer. Nothing elaborate, nothing flamboyant—just a plain old, simple request.

> *OK, honey. I want you to get up.*

Todd said,

I can't by myself, but if you help me I will try.

He attempted to do so with the help of a couple of men nearby. With that first step, all he could feel was the usual excruciating pain beneath his feet that traveled up through his legs.

The second step was as painful as the first.

But, on the third step, he felt like someone had hooked him up to 220 volts of electricity for a split second. The sense of being hit by a bolt of lightning pierced through his whole body. He took off running, managing to run the arena six times. To this day he is completely healed of RSD.

When Todd walked into his doctor's office back home, all he heard was,

Oh, my God . . .

Todd smiled confidently and said,

You're exactly right!

The only thing he required of the doctor was to put him in the medical journal as a documented miracle. The doctor graciously honored his request.

Incidentally, if you are wondering about the baby Peggy was carrying when she went into premature labor after their accident in Florida, she is now a healthy, beautiful little girl named Ashley.

Coming Forth as Gold

Why do we suffer? We don't have the answers. Joni Eareckson Tada, who has lived most of her life in a wheelchair ministering to those who suffer, says that God rarely explains. His answer is almost always,

Trust Me.

One thing is for certain. We have a promise for our future. This we learn through the Book of Job:

> *But he knows the way that I take;*
> *when he has tested me, I will come forth as gold.*
> —JOB 23:10

That is the promise Todd clung to in all of his suffering. Peggy said,

> *We had always prayed that God would use us to encourage and inspire people in their faith. Todd's working with Kathy is a fulfillment of that dream. But I don't know if God would have opened that door had we not walked through the wilderness first.*

What is the gold I see in Todd? He is filled with all sorts of treasures. And he offers them freely. He is such a kind and pleasant man. I don't know anyone who meets him and doesn't say, "He is the sweetest!" That doesn't mean he is a pushover. He is strong and will speak his mind. Justice is very important to him, and he will fight for what is fair. He is steady. He is consistent. I don't hear any complaining from him even on the hardest days on the road. He is peaceful. To him nothing is a big deal. All trials seem so trivial. I feel safe with him by my side. What used to put him over the edge seems so small now. He says,

> *My soul and my spirit are joyful. Just in the know-ing that God is truly in control—I am in control of nothing. The only thing I am in control of is my atti-tude and spiritual life. I must stay humble before the Lord. I have a calm in the midst of the storm.*

Todd and I will often talk about what the Lord has done for both of us. I believe it is extremely important in our faith to "reminisce" about who the Lord is, and what He has done in our lives.

Deuteronomy 6:5–9 says:

> *Love the LORD your God with all your heart and with all your soul and with all your strength. These commandments that I give you today are to be upon your hearts. Impress them on your children. Talk about them when you sit at home and when you walk along the road, when you lie down and when you get up. Tie them as symbols on your hands and bind them on your foreheads. Write them on the doorframes of your houses and on your gates.*

Talk about them . . . about Him. It is so vital to our spiri-tual health. When we forget to do this, it is like ripping an IV out of our arms. The very life of Christ runs dry within our veins and we get anemic and weak. Haven't you ever noticed a change in your reactions or your way of thinking when you don't put the truth of God in your heart? Or haven't you seen yourself get spiritually "numb" when you choose too often to be around people who do not love God? I can get a little lazier about gossiping. I am more prone to anger. I am far less patient and tolerant. And most of all I become a poor lover of people. The world is quickly perceived through my grid and not through the grid of God. I have sadly witnessed the change in people I once knew to be lovers of God. It can happen very slowly and subtly, but it surely happens. They end up exchanging their own philosophies and the beliefs of others for the life of God that once flourished in their souls.

We must not "forget to remember." We must remind ourselves of what the Lord has done and what He will continue to do according to His promises. Let's look at Deuteronomy again. There is a powerful message there in chapter 8. It was for the Israelites to hear, but it is certainly for all of God's children (emphasis added):

> **Remember** *how the* LORD *your God led you all the way in the desert these forty years, to humble you and to test you in order to know what was in your heart.*
>
> —VERSE 2

> *Be careful that you* **do not forget** *the* LORD *your God, failing to observe his commands.*
>
> —VERSE 11

*Then your heart will become proud and **you will forget** the LORD your God, who brought you out of Egypt, out of the land of slavery.*

—VERSE 14

*You may say to yourself, "My power and the strength of my hands have produced. . . ." **But remember the LORD your God,** for it is he who gives you the ability."*

—VERSES 17–18

If you ever forget the LORD your God *and follow other gods and worship and bow down to them, I testify against you today that you will surely be destroyed.*

—VERSE 19

Don't forget to remember.

I know a dear woman here in Nashville. Her name is Martha Bolton. She has written numerous books and is gifted with dry wit and humor. Some of her kudos are that she has written for Bob Hope and Phyllis Diller. What is special about Martha is that she has keen insights and uses words in ways that are uniquely her. One of the most moving things she has ever written is called *The Ultimate Biography:*

He was born in a stable in Bethlehem and was confounding temple scholars by the time He was twelve.

Though royalty, He never demanded special

treatment. No one rolled out the red carpet for Him to walk on, but He did walk on water.

Only one parade was ever held in His honor, but a week later the cheering crowd led Him down the very same street to crucify Him.

They didn't give Him an Oscar, an Emmy, or a Grammy, but they did give Him a crown of thorns.

He wasn't valedictorian of His class, but He was victor over death, hell, and the grave.

He didn't win a Nobel Peace Prize, but He is the Prince of Peace.

You won't find His face on the cover of weekly newsmagazines, but the book written about Him is the biggest seller in history.

He's not the Man of the Hour, the Man of the Year, or the Man of the Century. He's the Man of Eternity.

You won't find Him listed in Who's Who, but He is listed in I Am and He's the only entry.

He never ran for senator, governor, or president, but He is King of Kings and Lord of Lords.

His name is Jesus.[4]

"Am I not still God?" our blessed Savior asks.

Yes, You are God.

You are still God.

Part 2
The Shelter

Looking Up

Chapter 4
Always Present

Let's go back to that significant day in the chapel. From the moment I answered the Lord's question to the moment my mother was taken into heaven, He continually reassured me of His presence. It seemed like just when I needed a "Jesus touch," I would sense His hand upon me or even feel a "brush of His garment." He would let me know He was there. In small ways and in big ways, He made His presence known.

Blessed Are Those Who Mourn

There is a tremendous sorrow in losing a loved one, especially when they die before what we think should be "their time." Yet one sweet gift from God is when He gives you the chance to say good-bye. It gives you a chance to express your love and share the precious memories you had together. William Shakespeare said, "Parting is such sweet sorrow." Lots of times my mom and I cried, but many times we laughed as well. I remember the time my mom fixed pasta for twenty-five of my girlfriends in the heat of a Tennessee August. It was when I was first living in Nashville and everything was so foreign to me.

I was a long way from pasta and meatballs, and from hearing my relatives invite us for "coffee" by yelling across the backyard. My dear mother used to visit me in Nashville at least once a year. It was so wonderful when she arrived in town because all of my friends wanted to meet "Mama Troccoli."

I was talking to my mother on the phone one morning about one of her upcoming visits. Speaking of the phone, my mom never quite got the one-hour time difference between New York and Nashville (New York is one hour ahead). I can't tell you how many times my phone rang at six or seven o'clock in the morning. It would always go something like this:

"Heee . . . llll . . . oohhhh . . . ," I *would say groggily.*

"Yeah, Kath. You're still sleeping?" she would say with a shocked tone in her voice.

"Mommy . . . yeee . . . ssss . . . I'm sleeping." *Through gritted teeth I'd remind her again, "It's an hour earlier here."*

"Oh . . . I forget," she would say as she'd quickly go into conversation.

Back to that previsit phone call. We ended up discussing

plans to have a get-together for some of my friends. When my mom visited me, she would always bring some delicious foods from New York. This particular time, my mom went a little overboard. Not only did she come off the plane with three freezer bags of food, but there was a surprise she couldn't wait to show me as we emptied the bags when we got home. She had a childlike excitement as she unzipped one of the biggest pieces of luggage I had ever seen! "Look what Mommy brought for you!" she exclaimed. No, it wasn't a pair of shoes from Bloomingdale's. No, it wasn't a new blouse from Macy's. An overwhelming smell of onions permeated the air around us. The top of the luggage fell open. There they were. Bagels! She had packed about fifty bagels—every kind you could imagine. Although I missed those bagels from Long Island, that was definitely an anticlimactic moment for me. I think of that moment now and smile because it was such a sweet gesture on my mother's part.

The bags my mom walked off the plane with had all sorts of great Italian goodies in them. Pepperoni, prosciutto, ricotta, and grated Parmesan cheese. There was fresh Italian bread, mozzarella (it comes tied in a string), and cans of Del Monte tomato paste and sauce. The last time my mom had come to Nashville she was appalled by the fact that none of the grocery stores had any of "her cheeses" or "her pastas," so this time she was determined to bring her own.

During this season I was renting an apartment off of Belmont Boulevard. It was in one of the first high-rises ever built in Nashville. Except for the kitchen, the rooms were huge, and it definitely had a "romance" to it, but it didn't have any air conditioning. Long Island would always offer refreshing breezes in the summertime because we couldn't help but receive some of that ocean air blowing through our neighborhoods. That's what I love about Long Island. It is surrounded by water, and the water always brings a peace to my soul. Anyway, here I was living in the thick humidity of the South. Even with every window open and fans blowing through the rooms, it was hot and sticky.

My little get-together of "some friends" turned into a gathering of about twenty-five girls. Every time I invited someone, another someone would want to come. I'll never forget my poor mother sweating it out in my tiny little kitchen all day. She cooked and then cooked some more. Her lasagna and meatballs were the best, and I knew that every-one was in for a real treat. Even though it was a record-breaking 104 degrees, Mom slaved over the oven with a wet rag slung over her shoulder.

I had gotten a couple of interesting calls that day. . . .

> *Hey, Kath. Will your mom be insulted if I don't eat much tonight? I'm dieting.*

> *Kathy . . . I'm fasting for a couple of days. Will that be weird for your mom?*

I reassured everyone that my mother was not going to hold them at gunpoint until they ate enough. All would be okay on the mom front.

My friends came over that night. All twenty-five of them. All with healthy appetites. There was not one ounce of food left. Every diet and every fast was broken. My mother's gourmet dinner was quite irresistible. So was her personality. Everyone fell in love with her. That is a night I will never forget.

I savored memories like these during the year my mom was dying. I reflected on these times during the last year of my mother's life. My mom was a giver. She served well. I was lavished with her kindness more than I can ever recount. Because I knew she was dying, I had a chance to thank her for those times, to remember them. It was just one of the little gifts God gave us during that season.

And as my mother grew weaker, as the times of laughter grew fewer, His grace increased.

For They Will Be Comforted

Even down to the very last day of my mother's life, God reminded me of His presence through a precious African-American woman who was sharing the room with my mother. Her countenance was always pleasant and cheery. My mom was in and out of the hospital enough to have shared her room with what seemed like dozens of people. A couple of days before my mom passed away, the nurses brought a woman named Priscilla into the room and put her in the bed next to Mom.

Priscilla and I didn't talk much, and the curtain was always pulled closed alongside her, but she would smile at me when I caught her eye. On the day my mother was dying, I put my ear close to Mom's mouth so she could communicate with me. I also leaned in close so I could sing her one of her favorite hymns. My mom came to hear me sing at various churches, and she heard songs that were familiar to everyone else but brand-new to her. I began to sing gently, "Great is Thy faithfulness, Oh God my Father. . . ."

As I continued to pour life-giving words over my mom, I began to hear from behind the curtain,

Thank You, Jesus . . .
Bless You, Lord . . .
Praise You, Jesus . . .

Priscilla quietly prayed and praised. I began to weep. How tender of God . . . how intimate in details. To have this believing woman in my mother's room at the close of her earthly life was so kind of Him. It was definitely another comforting sign of the presence of God, a shelter in the storm.

That's not to say that the storm was not still raging or that there weren't days of frustration and a profound sense of helplessness. Especially when my mom was in pain. I wanted to do something. Anything to relieve the agony that I so closely observed. Sometimes I would pray softly and sometimes I would yell angrily. There were times when I would remain silent. Can you relate? We'll respond that way and our omniscient God is so very keenly aware of the turmoil going on inside of us. It's not like He says, "OK, I'll catch you later. You seem to be in no mood to deal with Me right now." On the contrary, His Spirit will prod us and woo us and reach out to our confused and wounded souls.

Isaiah 1:18 says:

Come now, let us reason together.

I love that. The invitation is always open to commune with God . . . no matter what. And the funny thing is that when we move an inch, He'll move a mile. In those desperate times when we feel like we don't have an ounce of strength to "come," He will gently pick up our heads so that our eyes can behold something—something that will keep His hope alive in us. We are never without a source of hope. He will always come. Jesus will reach for you in ways that will break your heart. And if your heart cannot grasp it at the time—He will gently remind you of it later. It grieves Him when you forget His amazing love for you.

I emerged from the chapel that day at Sloan-Kettering with swollen eyes and a weary soul. But when I got up from the pew, I knew I had left my heart in the hands of God. I hadn't even prayed for my mother to be healed. I'd just prayed that He would grant us a "knowing" that He would be there. I knew that if we did not lose sight of Him, my mother and my sister and I could really make it through one of the darkest valleys of our lives.

From the day my mother entered her room after that surgery until the day she closed her eyes for the last time, my sister and I read her the Scriptures. That was a crucial part of pouring the life of Christ over our situation.

Again, I have learned that if you don't give access to the truths of God entering your heart, many other "voices" will get your attention. Especially in times of crisis. We are so vulnerable. We can easily despair and feel hopeless. Our emotions are tossed back and forth like Ping-Pong balls. One day we're "fine." The next day we're "losing it." Even when we don't have the strength to read, or to put "good" things into our souls, we must somehow allow words of life to be spoken over our loved ones and ourselves. Obviously, the source of life is Scripture, but words of love could also come from a lovely book, a sweet card, or an encouraging letter. A prayer from a fellow believer could also be what blows a breath of life into our deflated hearts. The Lord comes in so many wondrous and miraculous ways. It's just that He doesn't always come in ways we expect.

Just recently I was invited over to my friend Val's house for breakfast. Her breakfasts are the "real deal." A breakfast at Val's is never simply cereal or toast with coffee. It will be the whole nine yards. My favorite: percolated Maxwell House coffee . . . lemon muffins . . . eggs over medium with crisp bacon and well-done potatoes. And there will be wheat toast and fresh fruit. My plate looks like a painting. I absolutely love it.

I thought it would be our typical time of catching up. But as we talked and ate, I knew the Lord had other things in mind. . . .

It always amazes me how Jesus is constantly aware of the state of our hearts. He doesn't miss a thing. We get bogged down with all sorts of duties that "just need to get done." We are concerned about how we look, and we spend a great deal of time on "our package." We worry about what success looks like and take pride in how others perceive us. We are consumed with all sorts of things.

And all the while Jesus waits.

If we are not consumed with God, we will most definitely be consumed with other things. Let me remind you again that we were created to worship God and if we don't set our affections there, we will easily worship something or some-one else.

My breakfast with Val was a welcome gift from God that encouraged me to "stay in the light." It also was one of those times when I felt Him reaching for me and letting me know that He wanted the best for my life. He knows how parched our souls can be for a touch from His hand, and He most certainly will deliver. Yes, the Lord comes to us in many unexpected ways.

I had been dealing with some of the responsibilities of "ministry." I had been dealing with some relationships that were causing me an extreme amount of stress. I was feeling attacked and heavy-hearted. There were storm clouds hover-ing over my head that I was either trying to ignore on some days or running from on most days. It was obvious to me that the Lord wanted to breathe His truth into my life in a way that would blow some of those clouds right out of my sky. He wanted to make things clearer and brighter. He yearned to reveal more of His heart to me. Val let out a gigantic sigh and started speaking to me with a gentle tone of concern, and I knew God was doing just that.

Kath . . . I've been praying for you so much lately.

The Lord has done so much in your life. . . . I've seen Him do miracles in the last couple of years.

Be careful. Be careful about your choices.

Then she said with a resolved shaking of her head,

To whom much is given, much is required.

The minute I began to speak, the tears that had been held back began to spill out and down my cheeks.

> *I know, Val. I am being called to an even higher place. It is hard. But I want to go there if that is where Jesus wants me to go. It really costs a lot when you want to be holy and encourage others to that same place.*

We prayed.

It was glorious. A weight came off of my shoulders. I hadn't realized how burdened I truly was. God knew. He met me. He had a plan.

God, Who Sees in Secret, Will Reward You

So often, we think we are looking up, but we are only looking for the praise of other Christians. I think that's one of the reasons Jesus warned us not to do our acts of righteousness before men, to be seen by them. It's so easy for us to shift our focus from God to man. The key to who we really are is how we act when absolutely no one is watching.

How many of us can truly say that who we are in public is who we are in private? I often confront myself with that challenge. We are so much better at putting on masks than we are at being who we really are. Part of that is because most of us are petrified at being "discovered." I'm not talking about those who wear disguises that allow them to lead double lives; I'm talking about the things that are far simpler than that. I'm talking about the freedom to express ourselves and our individuality without the fear that we will be perceived as "unspiritual" or judged as not being "Christian enough."

Recently I sang at a Beth Moore conference in Memphis. Many women drove from Nashville to attend this wonderful weekend. There is never a time when I don't get "my bucket filled" by hearing Beth speak about the heart of God.

Tami, a dear friend of mine, told me something the other day that really stuck with me about this whole topic of being real. A friend of hers, who is a baby Christian, attended the conference. She was supposed to go with a bunch of her close friends, but it turned out that everyone backed out. She ended up going with a group of women whom she didn't know very well. When Tami asked her about her weekend, she said that she had absolutely loved being at the confer-ence but felt uncomfortable around many of the women she spent her time with. Her exact statement was that she felt like she was with a bunch of "Stepford Wives." They seemed like robots who always said the right thing, responded the right way, and were void of solid opinions, extreme emotions, or genuine passions.

The women riding with Tami's friend all seemed to be caught up in the "should's" instead of being who they truly were in different situations and conversations. Their inter-actions seemed "stiff" to her. "Stiff?" I responded. "Yeah. Some people are stiff, and others are stone dead." I sometimes think the problem is that there are some Christians who define their faith with boundaries that God never established. They live without the freedom that God so deeply desires for us to experience.

Tami told me how the women had walked together downtown and had come to a beautiful fountain. Her friend had spontaneously taken off her shoes and let the cool water run over her feet. She told Tami,

> *Suddenly I felt a little weird. All their eyes were on me. No one joined me, and the conversation stopped long enough for me to wonder if I was being "inappropriate" or "unladylike."*

Tami has told me that her friend is really struggling with the authenticity of the Christians she is meeting. It makes me sad to hear all of this. Especially when I look at the life of Christ. There were so many times when Jesus responded in ways that seemed "inappropriate" to people. But He never pretended to be something He wasn't. Why do you think the King of Kings and Lord of Lords—the Creator of the entire universe—could bend down at the Last Supper and wash the disciples' feet? How do you think He continued to do it while these men argued about who was going to be the greatest in the kingdom of heaven?

> *He knew who He was.*

> *He knew whose He was.*

> *He knew where He was going.*

Galatians 5:1 begins:

> *It is for freedom that Christ has set us free.*

Yet we do exactly the opposite of what the next sentence says:

> *Stand firm, then, and do not let yourselves be burdened again by a yoke of slavery.*

We are so guilty of acting a certain way and saying a certain thing just because it seems like the Christian thing to do. Then we want the world to "come to know Jesus" and all they see is a bunch of hypocrisy because we can't keep up the charade. Our true person seeps out in an angry conversation or in a "vibe" we give off to people. Our true nature seeps out in gossip or in the way we handle a certain situation. Our "sincerity" is clear in the ways we are present or not present in others' time of need. The list goes on and on. The world becomes more disillusioned with Christianity, and the church just gets buried deeper in mediocrity.

On my own, I can't be real. I won't even have a desire to be "unmasked" if I don't continue to find out who I am in Christ. I won't live authentically if I don't give God access to every part of me. The church is in the same boat. If we don't allow the grace of God to flood our own souls, we will most certainly not be able to pour it on others. That is why so many believers are afraid to "come clean" with one another. We feel so "unsafe" with one another.

So often we can be weeping on the inside but smiling on the outside. But if we give God access to all that we have and all that we are, He is delighted to impact every inch of our lives. Jesus can also seem totally "unreasonable." That's why He says that His ways and thoughts are higher than ours. If you have loved Him at all, you know He is unconventional. He'll work in ways you may not recognize or understand. And He is big enough to do the things you have labeled impossible. He has enough power. He has enough time. He is bigger than your problem. Believe in Him more than in what you may see. Trust in Him more than what you may feel. You can question. He can handle your questions. God is highly confident of His own plans. He can do everything but fail.

Lord, the One You Love Is Sick

A story in Scripture that is one of the clearest examples of this is found in John 11. It involves three very close friends of Jesus and takes place in a tiny village named Bethany. The Lord often visited Mary, Martha, and Lazarus. Jesus loved this family. There had been many sweet times of "caring and sharing" amongst the four of them. That is why it was so incomprehensible to observe the choices the Lord was making when adversity visited His friends. But He had a plan.

The Bible says that Jesus had been preaching and teaching in the villages beyond the Jordan when He received the news that Lazarus was sick. Mary and Martha had sent word to Jesus:

> Lord, the one you love is sick.
>
> —JOHN 11:3

The Scriptures go on to say:

> When he heard this, Jesus said, "This sickness will

84

*not end in death. No, it is for God's glory so that
God's Son may be glorified through it." Jesus loved
Martha and her sister and Lazarus. Yet when he
heard that Lazarus was sick, he stayed where he was
two more days.*

—VERSES 4–6

Before we go any further, let's take a look at this. The message sent to Jesus contains these four words:

The one you love . . .

At that time and in that culture, I'm sure that phrase was used quite often and was a term of endearment for many relationships. In fact, it was probably very appropriate to address someone like that. But it prompted my thinking in another way. . . .

How many times has the Lord heard this reminder from us in desperate and tragic circumstances of our lives? I have seen it and I have heard it hundreds of times. I've termed it "holy manipulation."

Just in case God may not really understand the magnitude of our present situation, we refresh His memory a little bit. In this way we are sure to get a reaction from Him. You know—possibly push some buttons on the Almighty. Even sounds ridiculous hearing it, doesn't it? We have all participated in this kind of dialogue because we are sure that with love can come no harm. With love can come no severe injury of body or soul.

If You are a God of love, then . . .

How could a loving God let this happen?

She was such a good person. Why. . . ?

Basically, the question asked a million times a day around the world is, "What are You thinking, God?" I have heard Barbara Johnson say, "We think that the Lord has fallen off of His throne." We can't possibly fathom that He is aware of it all and in control of it all.

Let's look again at the story of Mary, Martha, and Lazarus found in John 11:4:

> *When he heard this, Jesus said, "This sickness will not end in death. No, it is for God's glory so that God's Son may be glorified through it."*

Jesus saw the whole picture. Not just the immediate situation, but the whole picture. We all have trouble seeing as God does because He looks through binoculars and we look through pinholes. He stands right next to us and says, "I see. I see. I know. I know."

And, as we arrogantly squint through our pinholes, we say, "You are crazy!" Prideful creatures, aren't we? The Lord has certainly had to endure my very own chastising remarks—thrown at Him when I have been absolutely beside myself with grief or anger. I am so thankful that He continues to rub His liniment of love on a heart that can be so abrasive—fighting to heal its own wounds.

At the end of the whole picture, God always has the same goal. The goal is the glory of His Son, Jesus Christ. He wants Him high and lifted up. We want immediate answers. He loves us too much to bring a fleeting gratification to our hearts that may cause a "momentary happiness" but has absolutely nothing to do with the eternal well-being of our lives. There is always a much higher goal. What we don't understand is that when Jesus is ultimately glorified, our souls will be at peace and filled with an unspeakable joy because we were created to glorify Jesus. We weren't created to "have our way" and "live our way." We were created to worship God and trust Him with *His* way. That is where abundant life of the soul will be discovered and lived out.

Yet When He Heard That Lazarus Was Sick...

Moving on in John 11:

> *Yet when he heard that Lazarus was sick, he stayed where he was two more days.*
>
> —VERSE 6

When we read this, we can be in a state of bewilderment as to the Lord's choice of action when He heard that His dear friend was sick.

It's almost as if we want a Batman-and-Robin response from Him:

> *Holy manna, Mary and Martha!!!! This calls for severe action! A super-duper game plan! Let Me*

*put on My black sandals, throw on My black
tunic, and jump in My black donkey-mobile! I
will be right over! To the rescue!!!*

Nope. That's not what He did. No action story here. No
immediate hero. Jesus did not delay for just a few hours. He
didn't delay for just a day. He didn't even begin His journey
until after two days! Why? Because He had it all under control.
He saw the whole picture. He knew exactly what was needed
in that situation. I often joke about the fact that I don't completely understand Jesus being raised from the dead on the
third day. I mean, why not on the first day—or even the second? God chose the third day. Why? Because He's God. He
always has His purpose, and we always have our plan. His purpose. Our plan. They are often at odds as we journey through
this life.

Let's pick up the story at verses 11–13:

> [Jesus] went on to tell [his disciples], "Our friend
> Lazarus has fallen asleep; but I am going there to
> wake him up." His disciples replied, "Lord, if he
> sleeps, he will get better." Jesus had been speaking
> of his death, but his disciples thought he meant natu-
> ral sleep.

First, let's notice the response of the disciples. They had no
clue what Jesus was talking about. Not a clue. And what is even
more interesting is that the Scripture says "but his disciples
thought he meant. . . ." We are always misunderstanding God.
We live in ways that question Him with the same statement, "I

thought You meant. . . ." Even our friends will be quick to tell us "what God means" when we're a little confused.

I remember when I was first told that my mother had cancer in her pancreas. I told you that the doctor had given me an estimation as to how long she would live. Do I believe in miracles? Absolutely! I believe that God Almighty can do anything He desires to do.

> *For nothing is impossible with God.*
> —LUKE 1:37

But that day I took what the doctor said to heart and gave it all to the Lord. I had some well-meaning friends say, "Kath, don't receive it. You don't have to buy into what the doctors are saying."

I'm thankful that a sweet southern friend of mine took my hand in the hospital and spoke words of comfort over me. "Just listen for His voice right now. The doctors told you what is going on inside of your mom's body; now leave it up to Jesus. He will guide you and give you wisdom." My mother had cancer. That was surely true. I knew my job was to continue to put her body, her soul, and her future into the ultimate care of Jesus Christ.

Look at what the Lord said to the disciples when they had summed up the situation:

> *So then he told them plainly, "Lazarus is dead."*
> —JOHN 11:14

Because of my experience, I'd like to think He was saying,

Look guys. He's dead. Let Me spell it out for you.
D-E-A-D. Dead. Let's not sugarcoat this thing.

Call something what it is and then let God be God in it. We are quick to put our own spin on things, but the Lord says,

> *Be still, and know that I am God.*
> —PSALM 46:10

Jesus Wept

As we look further into the story of Lazarus, we also see something that brings the heart of Jesus to the forefront. It has often brought me comfort in the most troubled and tumultuous times of my life. When Mary learned that "the Teacher is here . . . and is asking for you" (John 11:28), she ran out to meet Him. When Jesus saw her weeping and saw the Jews who had come along with her weeping, the Scripture says, "he was deeply moved in spirit and troubled" (verse 33). It goes on to say two of the most significant words about the tender heart of Christ: "Jesus wept" (verse 35). I suppose He cried for many different reasons. He cried because He was human. He cried because of His love for Lazarus and for the pain of His friends. He cried because of His disappointment with the things of this world. His intention was to give us heaven.

The Lord is extremely sensitive to tears. When you think about the fact that He created our bodies, doesn't it just blow your mind that He gave us tear ducts? We didn't even have to be put together in a way that crying was an option. Yet He gave us these little tiny holes for all that water to flow through. It is His brilliant way for us to dispose of our tears. He knew we would laugh until we cried and we would grieve with a wrenching far too deep for words, one that would have to come out of our eyes. Our eyes are the windows to our souls, and it is only natural for them to release the truth of what is being felt there. God knew life would be filled with moments of joy but also be laden with sorrow. When He was here in the flesh, He experienced all of life and all of the emotions we experience. He had feelings like us and He cried like us and with us. But someday He will wipe away our tears. I think that means tears of sorrow and pain. But He made our mortal bodies like they are because He knew there would be suffering. He knew we would definitely need a release for our gladness and a release for our elation. I'm reminded of a time when I was deeply touched by the heart of God toward our tears. . . .

A number of years ago, the 700 Club invited me to be the guest singer for one of their trips to the Holy Land. It was a glorious experience. To actually be walking in the places I had read about in the Scriptures over the years was so inspiring.

Jesus lived here.

He ate here.

He preached here.

He walked on water here.

He was crucified here.

He rose from the dead. Right here.

One day as I took a taxi, I asked the driver about some of my surroundings. I got goose bumps when he prefaced some of his answers with,

Well, in the time of Christ . . .

In the time of Christ. My *real* Savior. My *real* Lord. He lived and He still lives. The Maker of history will be the summation of history. I was in awe.

I was shopping one day on the street of the Via Dolorosa. It is a very narrow road with tons of tiny little shops. Trinkets and brass and rugs are displayed inside and out. There are many colorful images amidst the noise of the buying and selling. As I looked around, I couldn't help but think of Jesus. He walked this road with a crown of thorns on His head and a cross on His back. And I was told that the street would have been just as busy that day. There wasn't a solemn atmosphere. There wasn't a respect for the Savior of the world. No one gave a thought to the fact that He was about to pay for their sin while they paid for their goods. What I was witnessing was the exact thing that was happening on that road two thousand years earlier. Can you imagine? Amidst this holy scene I could almost hear the unholy chatter, if there was any at all:

Oh, it's that Jesus.

Always Present

Another day, another Jesus.

Why don't these impostors stop trying to be God?

King of the Jews? Ha! Just ignore Him.

I stopped in one of the many shops. In a display case was an assortment of sterling silver. There, in the midst of the bracelets and rings, was a bottle. A sterling-silver bottle. It was made to be worn on a chain. I asked if I could see it. Actually, I wanted to hold it. As I stared at this little bottle I thought of the words of David:

> You have taken account of my wanderings;
>> Put my tears in Your bottle.
>> Are they not in Your book?
>>> —Psalm 56:8 (NASB)

He holds my tears in a bottle. Our tears. Not one of them falls to the ground without His hands intervening to save them. He knew we would cry. He knew our propensity to sin. He knew the suffering in the world was not about to end with His walk down the Via Dolorosa. But He knew that as His life ended, eternal life would begin. He knew we would desperately be in need of hope. And He knew He would be that hope in our suffering. The cross would bring about resurrection for Him and for all who would choose to believe in Him.

I bought that tiny bottle. As I walked out of the store I pictured the few who really knew He was the Christ. The devoted. His true remnant. Their unspeakable sorrow was not in vain. Jesus would never forget their tears.

Haven't we often thought we were alone in our grief? That God had forgotten us? "He's God and He can do something!" we cry. Meanwhile, He is always "doing something." Even when He is seemingly doing nothing, He is doing something. A behind-the-scenes Director who is orchestrating a divine story. There is always a purpose. Always a plan. There is always the glory of God at hand, and His will most definitely will be accomplished. He feels deeply. He is moved greatly. He lets us bury our heads in His chest, and as He wipes our tears He wipes His own.

Do You Believe This?

To finish up the account of Lazarus, let's go back to John 11:23–26:

> *Jesus said to [Martha], "Your brother will rise again." Martha answered, "I know he will rise again in the resurrection at the last day." Jesus said to her, "I am the resurrection and the life. He who believes in me will live, even though he dies; and whoever lives and believes in me will never die."*

Listen to His next question in verse 26:

> *Do you believe this?*

Do you believe this, Martha? Am I not still God?

> *"Yes, Lord," she told him, "I believe that you are*
> *the Christ, the Son of God, who was to come into*
> *the world."*
>
> —VERSE 27

You can answer the Lord today. And when He asks again tomorrow, you can answer Him again. Your response will affect not only you but those around you. Will you become embittered or empowered?

Am I not still God?

Your decision doesn't affect whether He is or isn't. But He most certainly wants to hear your answer. Don't keep Him waiting. He takes great delight in your trust.

Chapter 5
Never without Hope

I read something very interesting the other day. It has been reported that approximately twenty-eight thousand Americans take their lives each year. December can be a very depressing month for many people, and a high percentage of suicides occur around the holiday season. The Golden Gate Bridge is San Francisco's trademark. This very well-known and recognizable bridge is also the final destination on earth for many desperate people. Since the first day the bridge was opened in 1937, there have been one thousand confirmed suicides. One thousand suicides! That amazes me. Not only that, but the bridge accounts for about 10 percent of all the suicides in San Francisco.

This is the part that really got to me: Reports have indicated that almost every person who has taken that leap from that bridge has jumped off looking toward the city rather than the ocean. Makes you wonder. Why do you think these people look toward the city and not into the deep, dark waters?

One last look at hope.

Their final picture, their final gaze, was one last look at light, life, and hope. I believe that as our hope slowly dies, our soul slowly dies with it. I have felt that kind of desperation.

Everywhere you look it is black.

Everywhere you turn there seems to be no door.

Every time you go to bed at night, you wonder:

How will I make it through until the morning?

A prison of hopelessness. Have you ever been held captive in that cell?

Proclaiming Freedom for the Captives

I remember singing at a maximum-security prison for young women. I watched the inmates file in through the gymnasium doors. My heart sank. Some of them looked like they were arriving for the first day of a semester at college. What did they do? Steal candy at the local gas station? I started speaking to God as they took their seats. *I can't relate to them, Lord . . . my life is the girl scouts next to theirs. They are in prison. They are probably going to say, "Who is this Italian girl—and what can she offer us?"*

Jesus said to me, "Oh yes, you can relate to them. Speak from your heart. I live in there."

Let the Redeemed of the Lord Say So

After my first song, I did speak. Words flowed so naturally and easily. I'll never forget those women listening to me intently. I knew I had their attention. "Listen," I pleaded:

I don't know what it feels like to be locked up behind bars.

I don't know what it feels like to wake up and not be able to do whatever I'd like to do.

But let me tell you something . . .

I do know what it's like to wake up in the morning with that all-too-familiar excruciating pain in my gut at the realization that I have to face another day feeling my own heartbeat.

I do know what it feels like to watch other people "enjoy life" while I feel like I'm standing alone holding a bag of worms.

I do know what it's like to question God and beat my fists toward heaven until I've exhausted my last ounce of strength.

I do know what it's like to feel utterly hopeless.

In that way we are exactly the same.

I think the most precious thing about that day is that I had absolutely nothing to give those girls. Apart from Jesus, I had nothing to give. The only thing I had to give was His life in my heart. The only thing I had to give was the hope He has given me and continues to give me. I could offer those women only what God offers me. I could lead them only to the well that I drink from. I yearned to lead them to the well where I find my comfort. Where I find my peace. The well that is filled with hope. It would be their choice whether or not to draw from that well.

Psalm 107 lists many of the prisons from which God has set us free. It is a psalm of hope, a psalm that gives us encouragement that no matter how deep our pit, God can free us. The key, whether we are in a maximum-security prison, a prison of our own making, or a prison that was built around us, is to thirst for the Living God. He is the One who is our hope. He is the One who holds the key to release the prisoners.

Why Are You Downcast, O My Soul?

Many years ago when I first moved to Nashville, Tennessee, I went through a devastating time of heart and soul. I stayed on a couch for three days and would not get up. I certainly wanted to die. Little did I know how present God really was. Charles Spurgeon said,

> As sure as ever God puts His children in the furnace He will be in the furnace with them.[1]

Friends prayed; I knew that they were placing me beneath the cross. All I could do was let the blood of Christ pour upon my aching soul.

Music was played that contained lyrics of praise and worship to God Almighty. Scripture was read that was medicine to every cell of my soul . . . reviving the deadness. Words were spoken over me that were like a flashlight in a dark closet. We have no idea of the power of words and their effect on our spiritual and emotional well-being.

> *The tongue has the power of life and death.*
> —PROVERBS 18:21

I was beginning to see again. That is not to say that I would never experience days like that again, but each year has become so much better. I can never live without the light of Jesus. I've got to keep in the light. Now when I sense the darkness, I must remember that the darkness is not dark to God. He sees what we cannot.

Every single one of us, even though we know Jesus, will have times of discouragement, depression, and even despair. David, who had a heart for God, frequently had times like that. What did he do? He talked to his soul, reminding his soul of the reasons it could hope in God.

> *Why are you downcast, O my soul?*
>   *Why so disturbed within me?*
> *Put your hope in God,*
>   *for I will yet praise him,*
>   *my Savior and my God.*
> —PSALM 42:11

We are told that David did this for himself—and he also did it for others who were depressed. He'd take out his harp and begin to sing psalms of praise to the Lord—and hope would return. King Saul had been abandoned by God (because of sin) and was plagued by an evil spirit. So, we are told:

> David would take the harp and play it with his hand; and Saul would be refreshed and be well, and the evil spirit would depart from him.
>
> — 1 SAMUEL 16:23 (NASB)

This is what my friends did for me when they came and played music for me, prayed over me, and spoke words of life to me. There are times when we feel paralyzed and cannot seem to help ourselves. Just recently a friend of mine came by who is going through one of the most despairing times of her life. She said:

> Kath—I don't feel like I have any hope to hold on to.
>
> I can't remember the last time I opened up my Bible.
>
> I'm disgusted with church and fed up with people who just want to give me clichés.

Most times God wants to burst right through all that. Often God will allow life to be spoken over our souls. That's why it is crucial not to isolate ourselves in times of despair. The typical response to despair is to want to hide in the dark, to stay under the covers, or to drown ourselves in TV watching. But that isolation just sends us further down the spiral, deeper into the pit. We are not allowing anything to come and buffet us up to the truth. We can't recognize lies until we know the truth. I know that in my own life, when I'm in that state and Sunday morning comes, I don't want to get out of bed. I cheat my spirit of the very water for which it is so parched. Or, the phone rings and my immediate heart response is: *I don't want to talk to anybody. I don't want to see anybody.* Those are the very times when we need to remain open. There are people we know who can speak "life" to us, and we must allow them to have access to us. We need to be willing not to wallow in the comforting bed of self-pity.

Some Drew Near the Gates of Death

I was at the height of "hiding" when I battled with bulimia. Nothing brought me more shame and self-contempt than the long, dark road through that struggle. It started at college. Before that time I was lean and ate anything I desired to eat. In 1977 I attended Berklee College of Music for two semesters. It is a very unconventional music college because its main emphasis is on jazz. It's located in Boston and at the time was basically composed of two buildings. Berklee was, and still is, a very prestigious music school, and I was excited to become a student there.

However, it was a severe change for me. There were no sororities or fraternities. It was not a "normal" college life. There were middle-aged men coming off the road to take a couple of arrangement classes. Students were extremely transient because many took just a course or two for what they needed to become better artists.

The female population was sparse, and I remember not wanting to go to the cafeteria the first couple of weeks because, as a female, it was easy to feel on display. Besides that, I was a Long Island girl who had extremely little knowledge of other cities or other cultures. I arrived there from "my little Italy" environment and was sort of thrown into a tailspin. I felt out of my element. I felt out of control. I began eating for comfort.

A Dunkin' Donuts shop down the block would give free garbage bags of all sorts of donuts to the students in town after it closed for the night. The guys and I would eat dozens of them at midnight and wash them all down with a couple of glasses of milk. On the weekends I was doing a lot of partying. The six packs of beer I was consuming were not helping the fog in my brain or the bulge building around my middle.

Most days I wasn't quite sure why I was there. All I wanted to do was be a singer. My mom was the one who wanted me to have the "education." "You could always fall back on teaching," she would say. I would want to vomit. I never wanted to teach. As valuable as teachers are, I knew in my heart that wasn't what I was cut out to be. I longed to sing.

So there I was. Pretty miserable. By the time my mom came to pick me up and take me back to New York for the Christmas holidays, I had gained twenty pounds, cut my hair, and had a bad perm. I'll never forget the look on her face when I walked out of the elevator. I knew she was thinking,

Is this my Kathleen?

I wanted to bury my head in her chest and say so many things.

I'm scared.

I'm not sure who I am.

I know I look bad, Mom. I feel bad.

What am I doing here?

What is life all about?

I didn't say any of those things. I was too prideful. My mom and I were at odds about most things at the time, and I didn't want to give her any satisfaction about my life being out of control. How sad.

I did go through a time of losing the twenty pounds and then some. I barely ate. I would live on a little yogurt and lettuce. I would often get up early, go to the cafeteria, and get an assortment of breakfast foods for my friends. I would never partake, but I would "watch" them eat it. Somehow it felt rewarding. I vacillated between anorexia and bulimia, trying whatever I could to maintain control—but actually I was so out of control. For months I starved myself. I identified with the phrase in Psalm 107:

[Some] suffered affliction because of their iniquities.
They loathed all food and drew near the gates of death.
—VERSES 17–18

I had gotten down to 117 pounds, which was really on the thin side for me. I still felt huge, though. The mirror was never an accurate reading for me. Those with eating disorders have trouble seeing themselves as they are. I was desperate to get thinner. I switched from anorexia to bulimia, returning to bingeing. I didn't choose to purge my food, but I would be desperate to "get rid of" my caloric intake. I never knew that taking laxatives was an old idea. It was all new to me. It became my way of somewhat "controlling" my "out-of controlness." I know this may sound crazy, but some of you may be thinking,

If it worked for her, it could work for me.

I'll just do that for a while and then I'll stop.

Not so. That is the furthest thing from the truth. You'll be stepping into a vicious cycle that will make you more miserable than you can ever imagine being.

Although I learned a great deal at Berklee, I didn't return after the spring semester. My mom insisted that I attend the local community college. It was in between my two years there that I dedicated my life to the Lord. This was definitely the beginning of my rescue, but I wasn't released from all my chains overnight.

I was still a chronic bulimic. I managed to stay at a steady weight, but that did not take the pain away from the fact that I knew I was in bondage.

I left for Nashville pretty soon after I received an associate's degree from Suffolk Community College. I was going to become a Christian recording artist. As I traveled down South, I took with me bags of belongings as well as tons of emotional baggage. The first year I was there I worked as a hostess at a local restaurant. There was that awful day when I called in sick for work. I couldn't get out of bed. It hurt to move. My stomach was stretched with food. My fat and caloric intake at that time was enormous, and my bingeing was a constant way of life. I would usually go from "salts" to "sugars." I would drive through Wendy's and then stop at Baskin Robbins. After that, a yearning for fries would spring up again so I would get a McDonald's fix. Chocolate, cookies, bread. I was insatiable. As always, I would eat a bar of Ex-lax and wait for it to work. I got to know which laxatives would produce the least amount of pain. I was a prisoner.

God is so amazing. Our gifts are irrevocable. He will use us in spite of ourselves, and that is just what He did with me. I had a thriving career, but I was barely surviving. Just recently I saw concert footage of myself in 1985. It was quite painful to watch. I turned it off fairly quickly. I was on the Friends Tour with Michael W. Smith. I was also at my highest weight and deepest anguish. Under my cheeks was a swelling from the laxative abuse. My eyes were dead. Looking at that footage, I didn't recognize myself. But I did recognize the pain. I remembered the chains. How thankful I was that He had set this prisoner free.

I was a public person but would often go through periods of extreme isolation. The couch was my solace. I didn't want to see anyone unless I had to. I couldn't bear to go to church because I felt so uncomfortable in my clothes and un-comfortable in my skin. Little did I know that the life of God was being squeezed right out of me. The only times I felt a little better or felt any "relief" were when I allowed light to come into my darkness. I wish I had chosen that "heart posture" much more at the time. It is so crucial to let our friends pray with us and over us. It is imperative to have the cleansing words of God Almighty seep into the pollution of our souls. It is "life" to our spiritual health to let any bit of His truth come into the lies we so easily cover ourselves with. They almost become a security blanket.

I'll never be free of this.

I am such a fraud.

How can I ask forgiveness for this again?

Then They Cried to the Lord in Their Trouble

Let me tell you, my friend. You *can* be free. You are not a fraud; you are a child of God. And God will *always* forgive you as you confess your sin. The only sin that cannot be forgiven is permanent rejection of Christ (because you are refusing your lifeline). But there is nothing, absolutely nothing, that He cannot forgive. You cannot "outsin" His forgiveness. You cannot "outsin" the love of God. You must know that it is the heart of God to set the captive free. We are all held captive by so many different things. Jesus can search out the deepest, darkest places in us. Not one of us is exempt from restoration or the joy of having a redeemed heart. It does take courage. It does take persistence. It does take a "wanting" for the higher things of God and a commitment to take the higher road to get there. The grace of God *will* always be there. Hebrews 12:15 says:

See to it that no one misses the grace of God.

He will give you the grace to change. He will give you the grace to be set free. He will give you the grace to believe Him.

He Sent Forth His Word and Rescued Them from the Grave

I moved back to New York in 1986. I needed so much healing. I got into a great counseling situation. Talking through my life every week helped me resolve some things. I took baby steps, and before I knew it the bulimic addiction was a part of my past. I went to a tiny little church during that time, and it was like a hospital for me. I was determined to have all that was mine to have in Jesus Christ. I didn't care that people saw me weeping every Sunday when I went to the altar for prayer. I wanted to be well. I wanted to be whole. I wanted to be His.

I'd be a liar to say I have it all together. Who does? I am still walking with some chains, and every day I'm breaking free from them. I want you to know that even though I am free from my bulimic behavior, I will have to be disciplined in my eating habits for the rest of my life. By the grace and mercy of God, I will truly work out my salvation with fear and trembling. We are miracles in the making if we want to be. It's our choice.

Let Them Give Thanks to the Lord for His Unfailing Grace

Many times I bow beneath the cross of Christ. I picture His head hanging down and His blood dripping from that piercing crown of thorns. His blood. His precious blood. Pray for it to cover you. Yearn for it to heal you. We are all mendable. We are all healable. We are all restorable. He *will* set us free.

Put Your Hope in God

We *have* to keep in the light. Once again, I know that in my own life I need to stay in the light. I won't experience the truth, the warmth, and the health of the Lord's light if I stay in and around the dark. It just won't happen. There's a certain comfort in allowing yourself to sink into self-pity or dwell on the unfairness of people and the injustices of life. But this choice only keeps you in an abyss without the hope and life of God to feed on. It's a choice to put your hope in God. It's a choice to trust Him in the dark.

Dwight L. Moody says:

Character is what we are in the dark.[2]

I want to be the kind of person who has a "steady" character. I don't want to be some flaky chameleon changing my spiritual colors according to who I am with at the moment. Sure, some things may be private. Like incorporating His life into your own. It's a process. And it's a sacred journey with you and the Lord. But displaying the heart of God? That is not a private thing.

We must be daily aware of living the life of Jesus. We should be conscious of His reputation in us. We must continually fill ourselves up to the brim with "good" things. Some of us read things, watch things, and absorb so much "stuff" that has absolutely nothing to do with the life of God—let alone His holiness. Slowly but surely it eats at our conscience like a terminal cancer and we experience a slow death in thinking like Him, living like Him, and loving like Him. Then one day we look up to heaven and say, "Where are You?"—and slowly we drift away from what He delights in and even live our lives as if we had never known Him.

A great Scottish preacher said:

> *The most profane word we use is "hopeless."*
> *When you say a situation or a person is hopeless,*
> *you are slamming the door in the face of God.*[3]

Don't slam the door in the face of the One who offers you hope. Your circumstances are part of a much bigger plan. I loved it when I heard the Reverend Billy Graham say something like this: "Each of us will stand before God one day. None of us will be able to point our finger in His face and say, 'You've been unfair.' It will all be made known."

I know I will be one of the millions of people filling heaven with exclamations of surprise on that day I affectionately call "The Great 'Aha' Day":

> *So that's why . . .*

> *I didn't know You . . .*

> *Oh . . . now I see . . .*

Why So Disturbed within Me?

When we are with the Lord, we will understand everything, because we will be face to face with Him. Now, Paul tells us, we "see but a poor reflection as in a mirror" (1 Corinthians 13:12). We only know in part. So life will often confuse us, often make us feel frustrated. Often our souls will be downcast. Mine surely was when my mother was dying.

There was that awful day when she lost all of her hair from the chemotherapy. . . .

My mother had the most gorgeous thick, black head of hair. In fact, in pictures of her taken when she was younger, long banana curls line her face. I would often tease her about the thin, brown hair she gave me. I would tell her that the only thick hair she "blessed" me with was right above my upper lip! It is still a morning ritual to "tweeze" my face. If I didn't, I could pass for a really cute pizza man.

I had to help Mom bathe because she had an open incision from surgery that was extremely slow in healing. It was very painful for her to move even in the slightest way. Both my sister and I tried to make her life as comfortable as possible. A friend of mine bought one of those white plastic lawn chairs, and we put it in the tub for my mother so she could sit down under the shower. I walked her to the bathroom one day to help her take a shower. How helpless I felt as my precious mother removed her clothes. Her body looked like the pictures of women I'd seen in a holocaust museum. Her flesh was barely clinging to her bones, and her beautiful olive skin was now pale and sallow. She shivered as she sat in the chair until the hot water fell onto her tiny body, removing the sting of the cold air around her. I tried not to stare at her. There she was.

My mother. My vibrant mother. The woman who fed me, washed me, and comforted me even on the days when I just had the "sniffles." She was afraid. I knew it, though she did not let a word of it come out of her mouth. It made me want to sob.

After I lathered her body and rinsed her off, I bent her around toward the faucet to wash her hair. As I leaned her head down to rinse away all the shampoo, I was shocked to see mounds of hair fall into my hands. What was left fell from her head onto the drain. I had a huge lump in my throat.

Please, God. Don't let me cry.

She looked on as every bit of her thick, blue-black tresses slid into the bathtub. She let out a cry that I can still hear. . . . All I managed to say was,

It will grow back. Don't worry, Mom.

The incision I was talking about earlier? That was one of the many times I got to see how much courage my mother held in her heart. At a time when most of us would complain, there wasn't a word. Not one word. In fact, the only thing I remember my mother saying about her condition was near the last days of her life:

I'm getting tired.

This incision wrapped around her stomach area. It had to be about two, three inches deep. She had recently gone through an operation (one of many to come), and for some reason this wound was not healing properly. For three long weeks I took her back and forth to the hospital in New York City. This deep cut that looked like a war wound around her middle kept on getting infected. The doctors said they needed to drain the fluids to keep it from getting worse. Every week we made a trip into the City. It was about fifty miles from our home in Long Island, and there never was a time without bumper-to-bumper traffic. The ride was so long and tedious for Mom. The bumps only aggravated her condition. I wished there were another way. I'm sure we would have done many things differently, but when you're going through something like this, you are operating in a fog. Nothing seems that clear. By the time we'd reached the hospital, she would be exhausted. I'd wheel her up to the particular floor where the procedure was to be done, then I'd wait outside a room, slumped against the wall, as I heard my mother whimpering and letting out cries of pain. They needed to cut open the scar again and again to get the infection out. They did it without any local anesthetic. I paced. I held my head and held back tears. . . .

Why?

Why Have You Forgotten Me?

When David was talking to his soul in Psalm 42, there were times when he seemed to be sinking, when waves of despair crashed over him and he cried:

> *I say to God my Rock,*
> *"Why have you forgotten me?*

Why must I go about mourning,
oppressed by the enemy?"
My bones suffer mortal agony
as my foes taunt me,
saying to me all day long,
"Where is your God?"

—VERSES 9–10

As I paced in the hospital listening to Mom's cries, I couldn't ignore the fact that this was my mother. This was the woman who took care of *me*. I remembered when I was a little girl and *I* was the patient. My mother was the one pacing, the one listening to my cries. I must have been about seven or eight years old. . . .

These Things I Remember

I often went to my friend Shari Goodman's house. She was my best friend at the time. Her family owned a dog, and I had known this dog since it was a puppy. Each time I was at Shari's, I did not hesitate to pet him or play with him. So when my mother, my sister, and I went there to visit one day, it didn't frighten me in the least that the dog was barking ferociously inside the house. They were scared and didn't want to go in the front door. I remember saying, "Don't worry. I'll go in first."

Well, it all happened in a matter of seconds, but as I walked into the split-level house, Shari's brother let go of the dog. I can still see his eyes and hear his bark as he charged down the stairs looking to sink those sharp teeth into whatever he could grab onto. I beelined for the pool table downstairs. I was trying to jump up on it to possible safety, but my little legs never quite made it. The dog jumped on my back and tore into my ear. I immediately held my stinging flesh close to my head and fell into shock. I could see the animal sneaking away. He was cowering—literally leaving with his tail between his legs. The house was in an uproar. My mom got a wet cloth and pressed it to my ear, and we took off for the hospital. I remember her sobbing, and driving like she was in the Indy 500. Little did she know that this was just the beginning of the gray hairs I would put on her head.

At the emergency room, a very kind and gentle doctor stitched up my ear. To this day I'm grateful to him because I didn't need plastic surgery. He was precise. As I was being mended, I kept asking about my mother. "Where is she? How is she?" The nurses kept on reassuring me that she was OK. When the doctor was finished, I was eager to get to my mom.

At that age I was about as tall as the gurneys, so as I passed the next room and the curtain was opened, I was eye level with the bottom of my mother's shoes.

There she was . . . lying on the gurney—out cold!

A nurse was with her, holding smelling salts under her nose. I just reached for her hand.

You'll be all right, Mommy!

And she was. She woke up and continued to mother me, love me, and worry about me for the rest of her life.

But now the story was different. We had reversed roles. *She* was in pain. *I* was the one pacing, the one worrying, the one crying out to God.

But even in the deepest watch of the night, the moon shone on the dark waters. Rays of hope.

For I Will Yet Praise Him

Our next-door neighbor in Long Island was a nurse. How sweet of God. She came over every day to check on my mother. She kept the deep incision as clean as possible and repeatedly changed the bandages. I know my mother felt comforted that she was so close. Those little gifts along the way are priceless.

It was the day before my mom died. I didn't realize its importance at the time, but it has become a day that has stayed in my heart. I have thought about it many, many times. I would arrive at the hospital pretty early in the morning. Mom would try to eat something but couldn't ever quite get anything past her lips. The cancer had steadily devoured her pancreas and liver; eating was such a chore and the last thing she wanted to do. She hadn't had an appetite for months.

Our usual routine was for me to read to her from the devotional *Streams in the Desert*. She loved that little book. I would rub her hands and feet with Lubriderm lotion. Lying in bed so many days had made her muscles atrophy and her skin extremely dry. I would try to be so gentle with her because of the "black and blues" that seemed to cover so much of her chest and arms. She was constantly poked, prodded, and hooked up to continuous IVs. We would also read the Scriptures every day. The Psalms had become her favorite portions of the Bible. She would often keep pencils in the pages and point to the specific psalm she wanted me to read. I was so thankful that my mother was receiving daily comfort there.

We spent many hours together during her illness. I had a lot of time for reflection. I spent a lot of time just being quiet. I kept a letter I wrote my mother when she was dying. I read it out loud to her a couple of months before her death. I dug it out recently to prepare for this manuscript. On most days I am overwhelmed by the difference knowing Jesus makes in a heart that has invited Him in. Without Him I never would have been able to even come close to offering my mother anything like this. . . .

9/19/91

Dear Mommy,

For the last couple of days, I have had a strong desire and conviction to write my heart to you. I know by now that you're probably not surprised at all that I would need to express myself this way—whether in words, song, or on paper. . . .

With all the stirrings of emotions I've felt the last year since you've been sick, I probably could write a volume of books—but somehow I feel led to write at least a small chapter, and let God (who is so knowing of our heart of hearts) reveal the rest of mine to yours.

All you hear lately are whispered "I love you's" from me, over and over again. Sometimes these words, although incredibly full of tenderness, can frustrate me because they seemingly end right after they are spoken. In actuality, they are felt deeply and I long to live into them every day of my life.

You have been and are a remarkable woman.

Even before you became ill, you were an inspiration to me, teaching me to love. You are giving and persevering. You always lived with the belief that "all things would work out for the good." You are a woman of courage and strength, and even now as you lie in bed every day, I grow by watching you.

You also know that there were many times I argued with you, slammed doors, and screamed cutting words. I clearly see my ignorance and sin. I know you have always wanted the very best for me and you tried to give your best.

You've heard my apologies, often through tears. I have tried you and I have hurt you. Somehow I feel the need to say again that I am sorry. I ask for your forgiveness. In many ways I have fallen short of what Jesus would have me be as a daughter. I praise Him, though, because thirteen years ago He entered my heart and has continued to reveal His heart's desire for my life. He has continued to teach me the ways I am to love. You have definitely watched me stumble and even fall at times, but you have also seen Him pick me up and take me that much further. I yearn to be a godly woman and move into all that He has purposed for my life.

I am in His hands, Mommy. There is no greater place for me to be. I know you are held tightly in His arms and there is no greater place for you to be. Rest in the love of His embrace.

Jennifer and I . . . you . . . we know Him. He's been so faithful to us. He has shown Himself to us and drawn us closer to each other. We can't ask for more than that.

I trust Him with your life. I trust Him with Jennifer's life . . . and I trust Him with my life. May His will be done.

Please know that I am so proud of who you are. I will always be thankful that I was brought into this world by you. This next season of my life looks promising. It is filled with hope. This next season of your life is filled with the same because Jesus is in our midst. Where He is, there is hope. With Him we don't lack for anything.

When I sing my songs, and when they touch the world . . . it will only be because Jesus has loved me and shown me His love. So, dear Mother, have you.

I cherish you. I love you so.

Kathleen

Mom listened quietly as I struggled to get through the letter. I'm so thankful for the times when the Lord allows us the chance to express ourselves. May we take every opportunity we can, so that we have no regrets.

He Who Dwells in the Shelter

The day before my mother passed away, she asked me to help her sit in a chair. I was afraid to move her, but she seemed intent on moving. I helped her up and positioned her comfortably as she put her Bible in the center of her lap. Because she hadn't eaten in so long, she had no muscle tone. Her body was weak, and it took everything she had to lift her arms. I watched as my mom opened the Scriptures to the Psalms. She was determined to read and read as if she were healthy. She turned the pages shaking uncontrollably. I wanted to wrap her in my arms, but I didn't for fear I would embarrass her. I realized that she had become my hero, and I knew I wanted to be like her. My mother said faintly,

Go ahead, Kath. Read.

And so I did. Psalm 91:1–2:

> *He who dwells in the shelter of the Most High*
> *will rest in the shadow of the Almighty.*
> *I will say of the* LORD, *"He is my refuge and my*
> *fortress,*
> *my God, in whom I trust."*

It became her favorite psalm. The whole picture it portrays—of being in the shadow of the Almighty—is what I saw my mom doing. You have to be very close to someone to sit in their shadow. The closer Mom came to leaving this earth, the closer she drew to God. She was sitting in His shadow. Though her pain continued, God was with her:

You will not fear the terror of night. . . .

For he will command his angels concerning you
to guard you in all your ways.

"Because he loves me," says the LORD, *"I will rescue*
   him;
  I will protect him, for he acknowledges my name."
He will call upon me, and I will answer him;
  I will be with him in trouble,
  I will deliver him and honor him.

          —PSALM 91:5, 11, 14, 15

I continued to read and she continued to listen, turning the pages with a dignity and regalness that left me in awe of her.

Deliverance for my mother was still a day away. That night was horrific for her. She twisted and turned, writhing in pain and discomfort. Up to this point she had not taken one painkiller. Somehow she held on to the fact that she had allowed my father to be given morphine when he was dying. Anyone would know it drastically helped to ease his torture, but my mom carried guilt about it. She felt like she had allowed him to be "doped up." Because of this she refused to be drugged. But after watching her suffer, I went looking for a nurse and asked that my mother be given something. She came to the room with a tiny white pill in a small "drinking" cup. I leaned over my mom and asked her to take it. Her eyes widened with adamant refusal. "It's not morphine, Mom. It's just a little something to help you. Please take it," I begged her gently. She did. Thank God.

Visiting hours were over. There was that eerie kind of quiet hospitals have after a certain hour of the night. Some of my friends, beautiful Christians whom my mom loved, arrived late that night—just to be with us at our most trying time. They were such a comfort to her. She knew they prayed for her and genuinely cared about her deeply. We all knew my mother had little time left.

When someone is that sick, they can seem to be at death's door and then live for two more weeks. It was so hard to know whether to go home or stay.

I left the hospital like I usually did. There was something about going home, getting into my pajamas, and taking the hospital smell out of my lungs that brought relief. There was something about eating some dinner and watching television as if my life were normal that comforted me. That night I felt horrible leaving. Something didn't feel right about it. When I think back on it now, I know my mother would never have chosen to leave me. But I chose to leave. I have often asked for mercy about it even though I know that God's grace has been given to me a thousand times over. I also know my mom would never hold that against me. Especially in her present state of paradise. Funny how we carry things, isn't it?

I received a call at three o'clock that morning. It was from the hospital. My mother was surely dying. They said she requested that her brother and two sisters be at her side. They had been her closest friends. Of course my sister Jennifer and I rushed to the hospital together. When we got there, we were told to stay in the waiting room. My mom refused to have us see her in that state. We honored her request, but it was excruciating. It was going on four hours when a nurse came in to check on us. "She's still holding on," she said. "This is crazy. You girls need to be with her." We walked down the corridor with pounding hearts. I didn't know what to expect.

The Valley of the Shadow of Death

When I walked into the room, it was as if I were visiting someone other than my mother. She was propped up on pillows and was an eerie yellow-gray color. Her mouth was puckered in a way I'd never seen before because of it being so hard for her to breathe. I moved to one side of the bed and my sister stayed on the other. I stroked Mom's skinny, long fingers knowing that the warmth I was feeling in them would soon be gone. She managed to talk to us. I would put my ear very close to her mouth as she struggled to get the words out. She loved red carnations and asked if we would have an arrangement made for her for the funeral.

Absolutely, Mommy. I'll take care of it.

After a minute or two, she motioned me to her lips again.

> *Order them from the florist on Carleton Avenue.*
> *He does a good job. Let my friend Janette take*
> *care of it . . . because then I know . . . it will be*
> *done "right."*

My sister and I just looked at each other with a knowing grin on our faces. Surely her two grown daughters couldn't handle it. We were still her little girls.

Time passed. I put my lips close to her ear and softly sang some of her favorite choruses. I kissed her forehead a few dozen times and told her that I loved her a few dozen more. She motioned me to come closer, struggling to speak. . . .

What is . . . today's date?

October 11, 1991, Mommy.

Your father and I were engaged on this day . . .

I marveled at what was going on inside her head. What a beautiful statement from a dying woman. Having lost my father so young, I was comforted by the tenderness of that thought. I loved knowing that she loved him.

A couple of hours went by and my mother was no longer communicating with us. It was very hard for her to breathe. She was gasping for air as her lungs began filling up with fluid. Friends and family had gathered in her room at this point. It was difficult to see her struggle. The nurses at Good Samaritan Hospital were so kind. I think it takes a special individual to be a servant to the dying day in and day out. They were attentive to her and never impatient. One of them came in at this point to check on her lowering blood pressure. She said softly to my mother,

Let go, Josephine. It's OK to let go.

I wanted to read my mother Psalm 91 one more time before she left us. I laid the Bible on the side of her bed as my sister encouraged me to read Psalm 23. I hesitated for a moment. I wanted to read her favorite psalm, but I promptly granted my sister's request and opened up the Scriptures to David's famous words. I don't recall having ever read Psalm 23 to my mom. As I stroked her hand, I began to read. I elevated my voice above the sounds of her breathing:

> The LORD is my shepherd,
> I shall . . . not . . . want. . . .

I watched with a holy reverence as my mother began proclaiming the words with me. It was as if an angel were opening and closing her lips. She "mouthed" the words with a deliberate passion. When we got to the end, she led the room of people who had gathered around her in the Lord's Prayer. I could feel the glory of God in the room. We were amidst the presence of the Holy One. My mother was not going from life to death, but from life to life. A supernatural comfort surrounded my heart. What is this life about if we do not have hope in a resurrected God who will also resurrect our mortal bodies?

The blood pressure machine went all the way to zero. My dear mother's dead body lay in that bed, but I knew her spirit was alive with Jesus. I leaned my head on her chest ever so lightly, and whispered,

> Good-bye, Mommy.

It was so strange to go to sleep that night. As I closed my eyes, I realized that my mother and I were no longer under the same big sky. I vaguely remember sitting at the dinner table with my mom and my sister after my father died. His chair would no longer be filled. We all felt so lonely and empty.

That first night my mom went to be with the Lord, I

asked Him to hold me as I slept. Even though there were a ton of friends staying at my house, an emptiness filled my soul. I had lost my mother.

I wrote a song that I purposed to write to bring comfort to those who have lost a loved one. Through my years of singing and speaking, I have heard thousands of stories about loss. I wanted to be able to express His undying love in a unique way and pour it over an extremely delicate subject. To say it hurts to "lose someone" is an understatement. There are no words for the ache. But we do have other words. Words from Jesus. Promises that are kept. We can hold on to the hope and certainty of our future with Him. It is not a forever good-bye. It is just good-bye for now:

> *I can't believe that you're really gone now*
> *Seems like it's all just a dream*
> *How can it be that the world will go on*
> *When something has died within me*
>
> *Leaves will turn, my heart will burn*
> *With colors of you*
> *Snow will fall, but I'll recall*
> *Your warmth*
> *Summer wind breathing in*
> *Your memory*
> *I'll miss you*
>
> *But there will be a time*
> *When I'll see your face*
> *And I'll hear your voice*

And there we will laugh again
And there will come a day
When I'll hold you close
No more tears to cry
'Cause we'll have forever
But I'll say good-bye for now

I can't imagine my life without you
You held a place all your own
Just knowing you were beneath the same sky
Oh, what a joy I have known

On rainy days in many ways
You'll water my heart
On starry nights I'll glimpse the light
Of your smile
Never far from my heart
You'll stay with me
So I'll wait

My sister and I shared vulnerably yet boldly at our mother's funeral. We each had stayed up most of the night writing a tribute to her and to our faithful Savior. I loved being able to stand up in front of my relatives and friends and sing the Lord's praises. In the midst of my sorrow were a joy and peace that could only come from Him. My mother was alive. My mother was with Jesus. I could tell of His love. I could speak of His faithfulness. I could offer His hope.

Surely Goodness and Mercy

You can put your stake in the ground today. Wrap your hands tightly around it and claim what is yours in Jesus Christ. His truth is ours to build our lives on. His life is ours to cling to. The hope of Him is our survival. His love is what will carry us and sustain us.

> *The LORD will accomplish what concerns me.*
> *—PSALM 138:8 (NASB)*

> *The LORD is close to the brokenhearted*
> *and saves those who are crushed in spirit.*
> *—PSALM 34:18*

> *Weeping may remain for a night,*
> *but rejoicing comes in the morning.*
> *—PSALM 30:5*

The happiness we desire so desperately in this life is not what God may have to "fill" our souls. He sees way beyond our circumstances. He can and will deliver a supernatural contentment and peace that are not dependent upon anything we may go through in this life.

Oswald Chambers said:

> *It is not our circumstances but God in our circumstances.*

He wants to fill our souls with Himself. With His life. Happiness dries up. Eternal joy abounds forever. That gift is only found in Him.

That's Jesus. He is our hope.

And . . . by the way . . . we do have a happily ever after. He promises it.

Chapter 6
Complete Trust

It was reported in the *Houston Post* that on the day before Easter, April 19, 1992, Madalyn Murray O'Hair kicked off the twenty-second annual National American Atheists Convention in Austin, Texas. There were hundreds of atheists there, and Madalyn pontificated boldly before the crowd,

> As long as there is religious slavery, mental slavery, we're not going to get anywhere as a nation. So, we're calling for the total, complete and absolute elimination of religion in American culture. We would not be in difficulty [as a nation] if we weren't being ruled by those classes of persons who believe in fantasy.

When asked why the atheists were having their convention on *Easter* weekend, Madalyn responded,

> We want to take back Easter and make it a celebration of the start of spring.

A placard carried by an atheist marching to the state capitol stated in bold letters:

IN GOD WE TRUST. NOT![1]

As I read about the course of events that took place in Houston, I couldn't help but think of my own beliefs. The people who marched that day are people who have absolutely no concept of a "God," let alone the one true God, Jesus Christ. The statement "In God we trust" is all over American currency. Yet it is mocked and ridiculed. It has been for centuries. The atheist has a heyday with this particular proclamation. I chuckle when I think about what would be put on our currency if an atheist had been our first treasurer:

IN MYSELF I TRUST

IN "WHATEVER MAY HAPPEN" I TRUST

IN LUCK I TRUST

The atheist can fill in the blank with countless things. But what about the believer? What about you? What about me? Can we honestly say:

In God I trust.

The Bible states:

Some trust in chariots and some in horses,
  but we trust in the name of the LORD our God.
                                        —PSALM 20:7

Do I live like I trust Him? Or am I tossed like the wind? On any given day—whether I am elated by the promises of God or suffering with the problems of PMS—do I trust Him? We are told that God Almighty will be with us in every circumstance of life, whether joyful or tragic. We have heard time and time again that "His grace is sufficient" and that He will give His grace in abundance at the very moment we are in need of it. But do we live like that? I'd like to give you a picture of absolute trust.

Recently I was home in Long Island. I own a condo there and love being close to the water and the Hamptons. Yet I'm just a short drive to New York City, where I can enjoy all of the magnificence that Manhattan has to offer. It has quickly become more of a vacation place for me. I love being able to visit my family without checking into a hotel. It is a welcomed break and a comforting refreshment for me to sleep in my own bed. I also love the time away from "the music business" and all the demands of my career. (Most of the time I reside in Nashville, Tennessee. There, I have what I need to do my business well. Plus, it doesn't hurt that I believe Tennessee is one of the most beautiful states in the nation.)

So here I was, wrapping up my visit to Long Island and being driven to the airport bright and early by one of my dear friends. It is almost routine that I want to stop for a "true" cup of coffee and a bagel before I head back to the land of turnip greens and grits. (What? You think I sound biased?) When

133

we pulled into a parking space at the bagel shop, we saw a big, black dog in front of the shop. His nose looked like it was stuck to the glass door. He was standing still except for the frantically wagging long tail that was attached to his rear.

Ever since my childhood experience of being bitten, I've been nervous around dogs—and this was a very big dog. My friend saw my worried expression and smiled.

I'll get it, Kath. Just wait here.

So, gratefully, I waited in the safety of the car and watched that dog. As people came in and out of the door, he did not budge. This dog didn't particularly bother anyone, but he didn't get out of the way either. A young man came out of the store and the dog immediately attached himself to his left leg and strolled merrily to the stationery store one door over. There he did the same exact thing as he did at the bagel shop. He glued his nose to the door and wagged his tail. When the man came out with the morning paper, the dog then attached himself to his right leg as they walked back to the bagel shop. He waited patiently as his owner enjoyed his morning coffee and paper. Customers continued to enter and leave, but the dog would not move. It was only when his master left the bagel shop that the dog followed him to the car. He contently jumped onto the backseat and he and his master sped away. For those of you who are dog owners, this story is probably a part of your everyday experience. For me it was a sweet lesson. A reminder of the Lord Jesus and His children.

That dog knew his master. He was not tempted to walk away with anyone else. He didn't want to go anywhere else.

He waited. No matter who came out the door, he stayed with his master. He knew to whom he belonged, and his trust was absolute.

In the book I cowrote with Dee Brestin, *Falling in Love with Jesus*, I wrote about a time when a former manager wanted me to sing a song with suggestive lyrics. At the time there were several influential people in mainstream music who were sure it would be a hit. I had to decide, at that point, *whom* I really trusted. Here were some of my choices:

> *Would I trust in the money that my manager was sure would come if I would just sing this song?*
>
> *Would I trust in the success he said was just around the corner if I would just sing this song?*
>
> *Or would I cling to my Master and say no to the above, staying as close to Him as I could, refusing to leave His side?*

I am so thankful to be able to tell you that I chose to stay close. And for a period in my life, I lost the money, I lost the success, and I lost that manager. But the One who really matters blessed me beyond all measure with His peace—and, eventually, opened the doors I have been walking through today.

No matter what comes in and out the doors of our lives, do we stay with Him? Are we convinced that we belong to Jesus? Do we know Him? Are we certain He is who He says He is? Trust. It comes down to trust. Oh, to have a divine confidence that when God doesn't make sense, we can trust Him beyond our reasoning. Just as Daniel did with the lions, just as Esther did with her enemies, and just as David did with the giant. They didn't necessarily have their circumstances "figured out," but they understood who their God was and to whom they belonged. Do we believe He loves us with a love that is always for our highest good? The Scriptures say:

> *If God is for us, who can be against us?*
> —ROMANS 8:31

If we truly believe that, we will choose to trust Him.

Choose This Day Whom You Will Serve

We forget that God is for us. We forget how much He loves us. Everything we question about the hardships of life, its injustices and its tragedies, should be processed through what we know about Jesus Christ. We know:

> *He left His throne in heaven in order to come to earth for us.*
>
> *He died an excruciating death to pay for our sin.*
>
> *He continues to intercede for us.*
>
> *He is preparing a place for us.*
>
> *He is coming back for us.*

My friend Beth Moore says that "the Bible is His autobiography and our biography." It tells us who *we* are and it tells us who *He* is. We can *know* who He is. We can *know* who we are. It is available to us. We don't have to walk around in the dark. But when the dark comes, we can hold on to the penetrating, persevering, stubborn love of God. The times when the inexplicable happens and we may not have a clue as to what God is doing we can know *Him*. He may not "let us in on" His plan, but He has "let us in on" who He is.

At the close of the Book of Joshua, Joshua asks the Israelites to think about what they know about God, based on everything they have been through together. Then Joshua gives them a choice to continue on with him and the God of Israel, or to turn back. He says:

> *Now fear the LORD and serve him with all faithfulness. Throw away the gods your forefathers worshiped beyond the River and in Egypt, and serve the LORD. But if serving the LORD seems undesirable to you, then choose for yourselves this day whom you will serve, whether the gods your forefathers served beyond the River, or the gods of the Amorites, in whose land you are living. But as for me and my household, we will serve the LORD.*
> —JOSHUA 24:14–15

Let's look at Joshua. . . . I love it when you discover a life-changing insight from an old story. That happened to me recently as I sat, enthralled, listening to a friend tell me about a sermon that had done that for her. It was a story from the

Book of Joshua. Almost the minute she explained it to me a light went on inside me that illuminated the fact that, once again, I don't have a clue as to what God is up to sometimes. We just want Him to act the way we think He should act. We want Him to prevent things that we think should be prevented. "He's God!" we'll say. "Surely He could have intervened!" I have said that myself so many times.

> *I wanted Him to stop my dad from dying.*

> *I wanted Him to stop my mom from dying.*

> *I wanted Him to stop my compulsive behavior and instantly deliver me from the pain of bulimia.*

> *I wanted Him to stop a guy who I thought I loved from leaving me.*

> *I wanted Him to stop my ex-manager from pressuring me to sing a song I knew was wrong for me.*

But He has His plans. His way. His timing. And so often, I don't have a clue.

We also have our own ideas of what His promises mean and how He should keep them. We have misrepresented Scriptures like:

> *I have come that you might have life, and have it abundantly.*

Whatever you ask in My name I will give you.

By His stripes we are healed.

How often the Lord asks us to trust Him! He longs for us to be strong and courageous. He longs for us to have an unwavering confidence in His love, His power, and His wisdom.

He *is* trustworthy. That's what we see Him telling Joshua in this amazing story I'm about to share with you.

Moses had died and Joshua had been given the mantle to continue to lead the Israelites into the Promised Land. Read on as God gave Joshua what I call an amazing pep talk:

> **Be strong and courageous,** *because you will lead these people to inherit the land I swore to their forefathers to give them.* **Be strong and very courageous.** *Be careful to obey all the law my servant Moses gave you; do not turn from it to the right or to the left, that you may be successful wherever you go. Do not let this Book of the Law depart from your mouth; meditate on it day and night, so that you may be careful to do everything written in it. Then you will be prosperous and successful. Have I not commanded you?* **Be strong and courageous. Do not be terrified; do not be discouraged,** *for the* LORD *your God will be with you wherever you go.*
> —JOSHUA 1:6–9 *(emphasis added)*

How often are we terrified? How often are we discouraged? And yet our God asks us to be strong and courageous. He asks this of us because our future is in His hands. Nothing will be given to us or taken away from us apart from His allowing— apart from His knowing. One of the greatest lies we can believe is that we are alone and that He doesn't care. He is so very close. He is ever present. He knows things we can't even comprehend. He sees in ways our human eyes could never perceive.

For the Lord Your God Will Be with You Wherever You Go

About two years ago, I was on my way to my yearly mammogram appointment. Usually I take a friend with me. I have found that it has been so comforting to have someone accompany me. Having lost two parents who suffered from cancer, I must confess I can have a "nervous anxiety" swirl around in my stomach during these annual exams.

This particular year I went for my checkup by myself. After my mammogram, I was in the waiting room area with a couple of other women to see if I could leave. For all of you "mammogramed" women out there—you know what I'm talking about. While you sit there with the "handkerchief" with which they have so graciously supplied you to cover yourself, they check the films to see if they got what they needed. It can sometimes feel like you're sitting in an igloo in the nude. Between my nervousness and my nakedness I found myself covered in goose bumps.

As I was waiting, I started to experience a deep fear. It felt like it was surging through every single bone in my body.

Will they tell me I have cancer?

Is this the day I will hear those words?

I closed my eyes and took some deep breaths. I tried to picture Jesus right there with me. I whispered His name over and over again. There is power in His name. It was so sweet of Him . . . a calming peace found its way through my soul. I lifted my head and truly realized that whatever news I would receive that day, I would have the grace to bear it. Not only that, I was certain Jesus would be with me every step of the way.

That week, I wrote a song called "When I Look at You." Here are some of the lyrics:

> *Lord, when I look at You*
> *My tears just melt away*
> *A peace comes over me and I don't feel afraid*
>
> *Lord, when You look at me*
> *I know I'm not alone*
> *My spirit soars above the pain my heart has known*
>
> *Hold me—don't let me go*
> *I need You—with all my soul*
> *There is nothing I will face*
> *Without the grace to see me through*
> *Lord, when I look at You*

It has been glorious for me to hear so many of the hundreds of stories the women tell me when I am on the road.

There is so much breast cancer. So much . . . There are many survivors and there are many who went to be with the Lord. But each story has had its own stamp of the strength and the peace that God Almighty lavishly brings to those situations. I have been in awe of the women who trusted the Lord, and I've been in awe of my Lord who provided the grace.

But let's go back to the Joshua story, because we are getting to the point that totally amazed me. When we trust God, it has to be His way, His timing. Trust, in the Hebrew, implies resting, waiting. . . .

In His Time

Let's move on in Joshua:

> And the LORD said to Joshua, "Today I will begin to exalt you in the eyes of all Israel, so they may know that I am with you as I was with Moses. Tell the priests who carry the ark of the covenant: 'When you reach the edge of the Jordan's waters, go and stand in the river.'"
>
> Joshua said to the Israelites, "Come here and listen to the words of the LORD your God. This is how you will know that the living God is among you and that he will certainly drive out before you the Canaanites, Hittites, Hivites, Perizzites, Girgashites, Amorites, Jebusites, and Termites [just wanted to see if you were paying attention!]. See, the ark of the covenant of the Lord of all the earth will go into the Jordan ahead of you. Now

142

> *then, choose twelve men from the tribes of Israel,*
> *one from each tribe. And as soon as the priests who*
> *carry the ark of the* LORD—*the Lord of all the*
> *earth—set foot in the Jordan, its waters flowing*
> *downstream will be cut off and stand up in a heap."*
> —JOSHUA 3:7–13

"As soon as the priests who carry the ark of the Lord. . . ." We need to pay attention to that "as soon as." How do we interpret "as soon as"? To me that means "right away." But not necessarily to God.

God is on a totally different time frame than we are. So often we have a plan. We have a dream. We have a desire. We have our eyes set on a mark.

God ends up standing on the sidelines watching us run this race that is going to a destination or even a frame of mind or heart that He hasn't ordained. Then we have the audacity to look up to heaven, with sweat pouring down our faces and bruises on our knees, and cry out to God, "Where are You?"

So often we get a plan and want God to bless it.

But then we are met with the "as soon as" timetable of the Lord. Time is so different to Him.

Do you realize that Jesus banged nails for thirty years until the Father said, "Now is the time"? That is when God's ultimate plan was set in motion. What He purposed since the beginning of time was going to happen. Authority and power would be given to Him. Miracles would happen. Words of wisdom and healing and comfort would be spoken. Life-giving words. Words that would be what we live on and put our hope in. Truths for which men would sacrifice their lives.

So when the people broke camp to cross the Jordan, the priests carrying the ark of the covenant went ahead of them. Now the Jordan is at flood stage all during harvest. Yet as soon as [there it is again] the priests who carried the ark reached the Jordan and their feet touched the water's edge, the water from upstream stopped flowing. It piled up in a heap a great distance away, at a town called Adam in the vicinity of Zarethan, while the water flowing down to the Sea of the Arabah (the Salt Sea) was completely cut off. So the people crossed over opposite Jericho. The priests who carried the ark of the covenant of the LORD stood firm on dry ground in the middle of the Jordan, while all Israel passed by until the whole nation had completed the crossing on dry ground.

—JOSHUA 3:14–17

What a story. What an awesome God. Did He keep His word? Yes. He always keeps His word. But He may not keep it exactly as we think He should. Let's look a little closer.

We are told that the Jordan was at flood stage. The river was at high tide and the riverbanks must have been running over onto the ground. We are also told that as soon as the priests put their feet into the water, *the water from upstream in Adam* would pile up in a heap. The rest of the water would be cut off and flow down to the Salt Sea.

The town of Adam was thirty-one miles away!

The water did pile up in a heap. Thirty-one miles away. Thirty-one miles of water would have to flow past the priests

144

holding the Ark of the Covenant. Can you imagine what was happening?

Joshua must have been pacing back and forth saying,

God, did I hear You right?

And let's not forget that the water was at flood stage. Can you just picture those priests with the water hitting their chins, with looks of panic on their faces? All the while thinking,

Did he hear right?

Is he crazy?

Joshua did hear God. And God kept His word. The Israelites just had to wait for thirty-one miles of water to pass. God answered. The need is always answered, but the process takes time.

I can relate to this so much. I ask the Lord sometimes, "Why don't You do something?" Like I said earlier, in reality He is always doing something. Lots of times behind the scenes. Working out my problems and working out your problems. Could He come into our lives in the way we desire Him to come? Of course He could!

But if He does not, it is because there is a better way. There is a higher plan. And all the while He will pour out His grace if we will keep our hands open to receive it.

When we choose to trust God, there is most often a period of waiting. It is amazing what the Lord will do if we just give

Him time. When we pray about something, let's keep our hands off of it!

> *I may not know until heaven why He didn't stop my dad, and then my mom, from dying. But I know that when I chose to trust Him, He gave us grace to walk through the valley of the shadow of death.*
>
> *Looking back to those early years in Nashville, I know He had a reason for not giving me "instant success." He needed to work things in and through my character that can only come through that season of hardship.*
>
> *I'm very thankful He had the man I thought I loved leave me. He was not God's man. At the time it was enormously painful, but the healing began when I chose not to manipulate, when I chose to let go, when I chose to trust Him.*

Sometimes we will wait a couple of days or even just a few hours, and then we'll go back to doing things on our own or doing things our way. Doubt and anger often brew in our hearts as a result of thinking that God completely missed the boat. Shame on me. Shame on us. We must continue to pray for humility, which is actually the ability to wait on Almighty God to move and act in ways He desires to act.

It was pride that made men ask Jesus as He hung on the cross:

> *If You are God, then come down!*

Could He have? Absolutely! But there was a more perfect plan. The story wasn't finished yet.

> *The LORD Almighty has sworn,*
> *"Surely, as I have planned, so it will be,*
> *and as I have purposed, so it will stand."*
> —ISAIAH 14:24

Here is another lyric I've written . . . after one of the thousands of times of questioning God:

> *I remember well*
> *The way it felt to look at life*
> *And find it strange*
> *If God was love, then why the pain?*
>
> *I didn't understand*
> *That You had never planned*
> *To ever have me see*
> *One day of misery*
>
> *And now I know it broke Your heart*
> *The times when I'd tear You apart*
> *Oh Lord, now I believe*
>
> *Love was never meant to die*
> *But still You gave Your all*
> *To keep it alive*
> *And I can't imagine why*
> *You'd give Your life for me*

But I've begun to see
That Your love
Was never meant to die

I've lived through tragedies
Those days I couldn't see
Beyond my circumstance
And leave my life there in Your hands

And many nights go by
You know I'll ask You why
Things happen as they do
But I have learned they hurt You too

Oh it was never in Your heart
To see me drowning in the dark
Oh, God, I've needed You

I think every one of us can identify with the words of the holy nun from Calcutta, India—Mother Teresa:

I know God will not give me anything I can't handle.
I just wish that He didn't trust me so much.[2]

It's hard to trust God during the refining process of life, but that is what God longs for us to do. Trust comes down to believing that God is good even when life is terribly hard. Trust comes down to believing that the One who is refining you, loves you and has only your best in mind.

He Shall Sit as a Refiner and Purifier of Silver

Some time ago, a few ladies met in a certain city to read the Scriptures and make them the subject of conversation. While reading the third chapter of Malachi, they came upon a remarkable expression in the third verse:

> *He will sit as a refiner and purifier of silver.*

One lady's opinion of this verse was that it was intended to convey the view of the sanctifying influence of the grace of Christ. She decided to visit a silversmith and report to her group what he said on the subject.

She went accordingly, and without telling the object of her errand begged to know the process of refining silver, which he fully described to her.

> *But sir, do you sit while the work of refining is going on?*
>
> *Oh, yes, madam, I must sit with my eye steadily fixed on the furnace, for if the time necessary for the refining be exceeded in the slightest degree, the silver will be injured.*

The lady at once saw the beauty, and the comfort too, of the expression

> *He will sit as a refiner and purifier of silver.*

Christ sees a need to put His children into the furnace:

His eye is steadily intent on the work of purifying, and His wisdom and love are both engaged in the best manner for us. Our trials do not come at random; "the very hairs of your head are all numbered" (Matthew 10:30).

As the lady from the Bible study was leaving the silver-smith's shop, the silversmith called her back. He said he had forgotten to mention that the only way he knows when the process of purifying is complete is when he sees his own image reflected in the silver.

Conformed to the Image of His Son

Becoming conformed to the image of Christ is a process. Each of us is a work in progress. Hopefully, when you look back at where you were as a baby Christian, you can see that refining has taken place. You are more like Him. Perhaps you can see that you are more patient, more caring, more peaceful in the midst of adversity. When troubles come, you do trust more than you once did—you cling to promises such as:

> *And we know that in all things God works for the good of those who love him, who have been called according to his purpose.*
> —ROMANS 8:28

So often, however, we fail to look at this verse in context. We think that the "good" means earthly treasure: riches, or health, or success. But do you know what the "good" is?

> *For those God foreknew he also predestined to be*
> *conformed to the likeness of his Son.*
> —ROMANS 8:29

The "good" is becoming like Jesus.

This takes a lifetime. And even then, the process will not be complete until we see Him face to face.

I know I am a work in progress, and there is so much that Jesus still has to work in me. But it gives me joy to see what He has done. I am gentler than I was as a young girl when I used to deal with anger. I am able to see people, really see them—not as insignificant, but as people with hurts and needs. Not always—but so much more than I used to. I have been freed from so many prisons—bulimia, anger, a lack of contentment over being single, and depression. Yes, every day is a choice, but I am seeing more of the reflection of Jesus in me.

The interesting thing about God is that when He sees that we are becoming more like Jesus, He doesn't say:

> *Pretty good. She's so much better than she used to*
> *be. She's still got a few nicks and dark spots, but,*
> *hey, there are other pots that need a lot more refin-*
> *ing. So, I'll just put her up on the shelf, turn her*
> *best side to the front, and let her rest.*

No. That's not what He says at all. He says:

> *He who began a good work in you will carry it on*
> *to completion until the day of Christ Jesus.*
> —PHILIPPIANS 1:6

And so we continue on, one day at a time, realizing the Refiner is going to keep working on us, keeping His eye upon us, but also, often, keeping us over the fire.

Part 3
Sailing On

Looking Ahead

Chapter 7
Winds of Faith

Without knowing God and knowing who we are in Him, we will constantly take our faith on a roller-coaster ride. It will go up and it will go down. We'll scream at the treacherous turns and close our eyes when we start speeding into a steep downward spiral. Trust doesn't change God, but it will certainly change the ride. Putting your complete confidence in Jesus does change the quality of your life. It affects your peace and it affects your joy.

It makes you able to endure circumstances that seem humanly unbearable. Watchman Nee said:

> *To hold on to the plough, while wiping our tears—*
> *this is Christianity.*[1]

Every day either He is God or He is not. How do we make that choice? What gives us the unction in our guts to pick Jesus? It is knowing Him and knowing who we are in Him.

155

I have seen many believers walk away from Jesus in times of overwhelming tragedy. I have seen some of my friends walk away from God when deep questions arise.

My friend Dee Brestin tells of a friend who seemed to be so excited about Jesus. She was the first one to arrive at Bible study, she seemed thrilled to be discovering this new life, and she was ecstatic about specific answers to prayer.

But a year later this woman found her infant daughter dead in her crib. The doctors could not give her any explanations, since "crib death," they said, "is still a mystery." Devastated, instead of turning *to* God, Dee's friend turned *against* Him, saying she couldn't trust a God who could have prevented her daughter's death but did not. Today Dee's friend is far from God, having returned to her old way of life, attempting to anesthetize her pain with alcohol and an affair with the man next door.

When there seem to be no answers, there may seem to be no God. We'll think, *He hasn't exactly come through like I thought He would, so I really question His other promises.* All of us have gone through different seasons of this at different times in our lives. I love what C. S. Lewis said:

> *It is quite useless knocking at the door of heaven for earthly comfort. It's not the sort of comfort they supply there.*[2]

So often God doesn't give us answers to our questions, but instead questions us. God is mysterious. He is also mercy and love. We must live in the balance of that fact. He is bigger than we are. He is wiser than we are. We'll acknowledge that on most "good" days, but when the hard days come, we can question His very existence. We must remember that we have "blind spots" and God doesn't. He sees up close and at the very same time looks way beyond what we can see.

As someone once said, we can't change the wind, but we can adjust our sails. How do we adjust our sails? By remembering what we know about Him.

I Know Whom I Have Believed

We must be certain of who He is. We must be certain of His character. I have had the blessing of having incredible friends in my life. They have provided for me, cared for me, and comforted me. They have prayed for me and loved me in ways I will be thankful for far into eternity. Many times I have seen firsthand that love "believes the best." I have also seen how love "covers" and protects. Recently a conversation took place between one of my dear friends and a business associate of hers. I had never met this person. My friend listened as this woman talked about me, "quoted" me, and insisted that I said something I did not. As this person got to the end of her assessment of my character, my friend confidently and kindly responded with these words:

> *I know Kathy Troccoli. I know her very well. She would never ever say something like that. And . . . according to what I know about what she believes and stands for, she would never make a statement like that. Never.*

In the same way, when things happen in our lives that don't make sense and others want to accuse God of wrongdoing (remember Job's wife, who told him, "Curse God and die!"), we have to rest on the character of God and His history of faithfulness. God may not explain. He may not reveal His plan. But He has revealed Himself. All our doubts about God and suffering should be filtered through what we know about Jesus. And, based on our knowing God and His character, we can say, with confidence:

> He has *a plan for my future that is good and not evil.*

> He will *never leave me or forsake me.*

> He loves *me with an undying love. It is penetrating, persevering, and stubborn.*

> He is *faithful to forgive my sins.*

> He will *keep His promises.*

The Scriptures say in 2 Peter 3:18:

> But *grow in the grace and knowledge of our Lord and Savior Jesus Christ.*

You must also remember who you are to Him. Remind yourself every day who you are in Him. It will give you a holy confidence. Thelma Wells has said that God has one weakness. It is a weak spot for you.

I am His child.

I belong to Him.

I am His beloved.

I am a conqueror.

I am precious in His sight.

So leave little room for doubt. Make a way for hope. Know who He is. And know who you are.

Jesus was the epitome of "knowing who He was." Picture this. At the Last Supper, while the disciples were arguing about who was going to be the greatest in the kingdom of heaven, what was Jesus doing? He was washing their feet! How could He do this? He knew who He was. He knew why He came. He knew His Father was sufficient to meet His deepest needs.

We all have a craving for affirmation. It's only human. We were created with all kinds of "soul" needs. Jesus is the only one fitted to meet them. Do we really grasp this?

It is also interesting that during the Last Supper Jesus told His disciples that they didn't know what He was doing but later they would know. That is a pattern I have learned about my Lord.

Later we will know.

Even if the final "later" is in heaven, we will know. It *will* be revealed.

Martin Luther said:

Man hides his own things in order to conceal them;
God hides His own things in order to reveal them.[3]

Matthew 6:6 says:

But when you pray, go into your room, close the
door and pray to your Father, who is unseen.
Then your Father, who sees what is done in secret,
will reward you.

There are two key words here. *Unseen* and *secret*. This is what Jesus asks us to do. Pray to our Father who is unseen, who sees what is done in secret. These words are mentioned clearly. Jesus works through and in the unseen and the secret. Some of us would like Him to hold a press conference so we could understand what He is doing. We want to understand clearly and know immediately. It is just in our nature. But it is not in His nature to do so. Look at how He handled His own Deity. He didn't walk around with a sign on His back that said,

I AM THE SON OF GOD

He just was. He just is. He lived on this earth and He can live in our hearts. Unseen but known. Knowing secrets but holding them close to His heart. He knows what we can handle. He knows the right time for "revelation." We have to trust Him to hold the answers until He decides to boldly display them before our eyes.

Each one of us is encouraged when we look at the lives of those who have sailed on successfully and victoriously, even in the most treacherous of waters. People who have been up against tidal waves and hurricanes. Their needs were great and they met them with Jesus. If we are honest, we'll admit that so often we walk around with a cup in our hands, saying, "Is there anyone out there who can fill my cup?" All the while Jesus is waiting for us to find our fulfillment in Him. Everything else should be the overflow.

Helping One Another Find Strength in God

I enjoy getting to speak and sing to women all over the world. These have been some of the most beautiful times of my life. That is not to say I don't like to sing to men and children also. I am thankful for it all. It just seems that in the last couple of years, the Lord has definitely been opening doors for me to impact the lives of women.

I hear all sorts of stories. I am asked to pray for many things. I count it all as such a privilege. There have been many times when I will be at the autograph table for as long as I have been onstage. It is so important for me to connect with the people.

There have been many times that an "exchange" will bless me just as much as it blesses the person wanting to converse with me. Recently at the autograph table I was told about a woman named Jody who was extremely ill. As her friend told me about Jody's suffering, I felt compelled to ask if I could call her. Her friend said that some days were very difficult so she didn't know if I could actually speak with her but that I could certainly try. As people waited in line, I called Jody on her friend's cell phone.

How warmed I was by Jody's grace and demeanor. I thought I was calling to "bless" her, when in actuality, I ended up encountering my Savior. The person of Christ was living in Jody in such an obviously powerful way. It was so evident to me. I ended up getting this e-mail some time later:

> Hello Kathy,
>
> My name is Amanda. I met you at your table in Minneapolis. I shared briefly about my friend Jody who is dying of AIDS. You amazingly offered to call her to pray. I cannot even tell you what that meant to her. She was so touched. She could hardly wait to talk to me after the conference to ask all about you. I wanted to share a little more about her story and will keep you updated as often as you would like.
>
> Jody and I grew up together in Cedar Rapids, Iowa. After graduation she left for the University of Kansas. Upon returning to school after Christmas break that year, she was brutally raped by a classmate. It was a guy she met in class. They were in a study group together. He was a "Christian" with a girlfriend back home. He had asked her out shortly before the holiday break, and she had turned him down. She was committed to John, her boyfriend back home.
>
> Jody and John were waiting until marriage to consummate their relationship. She was a virgin.

Apparently enraged by this, this boy who had been pursuing her attacked her, and then threatened to take her life and John's life if she told anyone.

Jody left school shortly after this incident, as she was too terrified to stay there. She enrolled in a school in our hometown that next fall. John was helping her put her life back together. She went through a great deal of therapy. A year and a half later, she received a phone call from this boy's cousin, telling her that he was in the hospital dying of AIDS, and that she should be tested.

She tested positive.

John married her, despite this. He is her caregiver to this day. This January will have been eleven years since the attack. Solely the Lord sustains her. She has not eaten in almost a year; she has refused hospitalization and remained home throughout her illness. She speaks to young people on her good days and witnesses from the couch on bad ones. She has not been able to sit up for a full year. She is as determined as ever to share God's love with everyone. Sadly, it has taken us until last year to get through to her husband, who is now growing in his faith more every day. Her entire family is still rejecting the very witness that lays before them. I am her only Christian friend, and my parents, who still live there, continue to share and minister to her, and allow her to minister to them.

Jody longs to win the world to Christ. She is not bitter. She is not sad. She endures pain beyond anything we can imagine. She has cancer throughout her entire body. Doctors told her years ago that there is no medical reason for her to be alive. The tumors in her brain are so large that she suffers from seizures constantly. Her body has been ravished by every illness/disease/ infection you've ever heard of. Yet she smiles and tells people that God is love.

She has forgiven the boy who did this to her. She loves. She has truly "lit" her corner of the world.

Kathy, your music is all she has some days. She takes so much morphine to tolerate the amount of pain she is in that many days she cannot talk. But she can hear. She lives with her headphones on, and plays the tape I made for her of your music. She lives out the song "How Would I Know?"

I just wanted you to know how you have brought a little "light" into the life of my friend. Thank you so much for your music, and for your prayer on the phone with her.

We love you.

Remarkable. Just remarkable. The Bible says that the Spirit that raised Christ from the dead lives in us. What a testimony to the fact that God will give His Spirit without boundaries to anyone who allows Him freedom to do so.

Suffering. As long as we are under this great big sky, there will be suffering. But rest assured that when you suffer as a Christian, your suffering is not in vain.

I've had the repeated pleasure of singing at the women's conference called The Heritage Keepers. There are many times at these events when I choose to sit in the audience with the rest of the women who are attending. I take my little black notebook and scribble notes fast and furiously throughout the whole day. I want to learn. I want to bask in the wisdom and knowledge that these speakers have acquired in serving Jesus. One day I glanced at my program after lunch to see who was about to take the platform. Her name was Renee Bondi. *Hmm . . . never heard of her,* I thought. Boy, was I in for a life-changing experience. She was introduced, and a cherub-faced, sweet-spirited woman wheeled herself onto the stage. She had a smile that could melt the moon and was singing,

> *Be not afraid. I go before you always. Come follow Me . . . and I will give you rest.*

Her countenance was angelic. I immediately felt closer to Jesus. So many thoughts ran through my head:

> *Can I have that kind of love for Him?*

> *I want to glow like that when I am on the stage.*

> *There is such beauty in a woman who is in love with Jesus.*

She finished the song and began to tell her story. In 1988 she fell out of bed in the middle of the night. It was a freak accident. Her head hit the floor in a way that left her paralyzed. She was to be married within two months. I listened in amazement as she went on to share about that season in her life. She talked about the incredible love of God and His supernatural presence in her life. Did she deal with doubt and depression? She most definitely did. But one night, months into her hospital stay, she was praying and felt God reassure her. The words to a hymn she had known her whole life kept ringing in her mind. It was the song she was singing when she came out on the stage:

> *Be not afraid. I go before you always. Come follow Me . . . and I will give you rest.*

I started to cry as she went on to say that the Lord was speaking to her. She realized that she was going to get through it. She said,

> *I knew I was going to be OK—but I also knew the definition of "OK" had radically changed.*

She went on to say that her fiancé, Mike, stayed right by her side. He married her and they were able to have a son, named Daniel. Before the accident she was a choral teacher, and with hard work and determination she was able to get her voice back. What a testimony. What a life. Jesus was so tangible in this woman.

I invited her to sing "Go Light Your World" with me during my segment. It brought the house down. I was convinced that the glory of God filled the room. You couldn't help but sense the hope that was being revived in the heart of every woman there. Renee exchanged her grief for the glory of God. I had a feeling that the women around that auditorium were doing the same.

> *For our light and momentary troubles are achieving*
> *for us an eternal glory that far outweighs them all.*
> —2 CORINTHIANS 4:17

If We Share in His Sufferings, We Will Share in His Glory

The apostle Paul tells us in Romans 8:17:

> *Now if we are children, then we are heirs—heirs*
> *of God and co-heirs with Christ, if indeed we share*
> *in his sufferings in order that we may also share in*
> *his glory.*

Amanda mentioned the song "How Would I Know?" I can't tell you how many people have told me how that song has carried them through some really dark times.

I was in California recording my project "Love and Mercy." The musicians and singers were all on a lunch break, and I was sitting on a chair just taking a breather. My producer asked one of the background singers, Jackie Gouché-Ferris, to play me a song. He said it was an incredible lyric. I moved over to the baby grand piano that was nearby. This beautiful woman began to play and sing her heart out. I was immediately drawn in the minute she opened her mouth. I knew I had lived this lyric, and felt this lyric. She wasn't even halfway through the first verse when I started to cry:

> *If it wasn't for the times that I was down*
> *If it wasn't for the times that I was bound*
> *For all the times that I wondered*
> *How I could ever make it through*
> *All of the times that I couldn't see my way*
> *And I had to turn to You . . .*
>
> *How would I know You could deliver?*
> *How would I know You could set free?*
> *If there had never been a battle*
> *How would I know the victory?*
> *How would I know You could be faithful,*
> *To meet all of my needs?*
> *Lord, I appreciate the hard times*
> *Otherwise how would I know?*
>
> *I remember all the times I had to cry*
> *And at the time all I could do was wonder why.*
> *Why would a God so kind and loving*
> *Allow me to go through all this pain?*
> *If I could see into the future*
> *Then I would know the joy I'd gain. . . .*

When I moved to Nashville in 1980, I lived in a room above the garage of a home that belonged to my manager and his family. They were gracious enough to provide a place for me to live until I could afford my own apartment. Before I left for Tennessee, my closest friends threw me a going-away party. Everyone seemed to be so encouraged about my "promising" future. It was an exciting time. I was definitely the big fish in the small pond in Long Island. I was the Christian singer who had potential to "make it big."

I woke up one morning about two weeks after I had moved to Nashville with a heavy heart. The house was empty and so was my soul. The reality was that a recording contract was going to take time, if I was going to get one at all. It seemed like a million miles away. It was a dream that was far out of my reach. I felt so lonely, so discouraged, and I started to second-guess everything.

What was I thinking?

What am I doing here?

Did I do the right thing?

I decided to take a walk. I didn't know my way around at all, but I just started walking. My manager's "harmless" chocolate Labrador seemed eager to follow me, so I let him. What a picture that was. I looked at him and then looked at myself. I couldn't help but smile inside. I am for the most part a New York kind of girl, but at that moment I felt so earthy. It was like I was in a Kodak commercial. All I needed was "The Times of Your Life" playing in the background.

I happened upon a long road that was lined with tall, old trees and white fences. It was beautiful. It was a breezy day, and I felt that tinge of cool upon my face. Leaves covered the ground like a blanket, and I knew this road was probably stunning in the height of the fall and spring. Now it was completely barren. The scene before me and around me was symbolic of what I felt like inside. I knew deep down that this was just the beginning of a long journey of seasons where I would walk through a dying process. I knew that the Lord was showing me a picture of what many of the days ahead would look like. I also knew that there is never a spring without a fall. Without death there wouldn't be life. And there would always be life if I waited for it.

Take a picture of a healthy tree in the prime season of summer. The brilliance of the colors can be breathtaking. There is vibrancy. There is growth. There is life. Look at the same tree in the height of fall. Empty. Stripped. Alive on the inside but dead on the outside.

How true it is for us as God's children. In this life our flesh may be dying, our circumstances may leave us feeling stripped of our pride or dignity, and our lives may seem empty of any promise. But the Spirit that raised Jesus from the dead lives inside of us! We are never without the life of God. We are never without hope. It is always within our grasp. We are never without the certainty of His promises. They are always there for us to build our lives upon.

I didn't have a record out until two years after I moved to Nashville. The move to Nashville was just the beginning of my story. The Lord wanted to teach me many things about myself and many things about Him. He cared about my future and He cared about my dreams. He was far more concerned with the condition of my heart. What were the circumstances that I found myself in?

Bad relationships.

Frustrating management decisions or the lack thereof.

Poor "life management."

Endless days on the road.

Disappointments.

Lack of results.

I often found myself feeling the worst when people thought I was flying high. I didn't ever feel like I was really doing anything of significance. I constantly compared myself to other artists. I wondered if I was God's stepchild and not His "real" child. I never quite felt like I would ever find a groove for my life that would allow me to flow with any kind of ease.

For some of us, this "state of heart" can last for weeks. For others, months. And for people like me, it can last for years. I must tell you that it has all been used to allow me to receive God's best. It has been used to continue to get me to "look up." It has been used to let me know that my self-worth is found only in Him and in nothing else. It has been used to allow His dreams for me to truly become the dreams I would have for myself. He wants His concerns to be my concerns. He wants His priorities to be my priorities. I'll share more about this later.

Let God have His way. Give it all to Him. You will be

amazed one day when He rolls the stone away from the tomb of your agendas. You will see it empty. It held your plans, your perspective, and your wisdom. He will then allow you to live into a glorious resurrection. You will fulfill His purpose.

> *If I rise on the wings of the dawn,*
> *if I settle on the far side of the sea,*
> *even there your hand will guide me,*
> *your right hand will hold me fast.*
>
> *If I say, "Surely the darkness will hide me*
> *and the light become night around me,"*
> *even the darkness will not be dark to you.*
> —PSALM 139:9–12

Even in the most raging waters, our Lord's hand will guide us and will hold us fast. Even in our darkest moments, the Lord is illuminating and clear. We often wonder, "Do You know what You're doing?" Yes, He does. We can be sure of it. God speaks to us often and says,

Let Me worry about that.

The Bible says continually that He knows the plans He has for us, and they are for our good and not for our demise. Jesus will always come between us and our sorrow, between us and our fear, between us and our pain. We cannot get away from God. If you continue to read through Psalm 139, you'll see that it is revelatory!

When we feel like we are spinning out of control
He has hemmed us in—behind and before

When we're restless and we can't sleep
He knows when we sit and when we rise

In times of elation and joy
If we go to the heavens, He is there

In times of depression and despair
If we make our bed in the depths, He is there

When we experience peace and fulfillment
If we rise on the wings of the dawn, He is there

When we are uprooted
If we settle on the far side of the sea, He is there

Our precious Jesus will meet extraordinary pain with extraordinary grace. He will meet extraordinary needs with extraordinary resources. He will meet extraordinary fears with extraordinary comfort. And although the Lord does care about our deepest needs and is concerned with the details of our lives, He is always on a quest for our hearts. Our faith is what is of interest to Him. It isn't our circumstances. It's the building up of our faith. I heard this statement recently:

> *His goal is not necessarily to make us happy. His goal is to make us His.*

There are thousands of times when we'll ask God what He is doing to us. We must be more concerned with what He wants to do in us. I am talking about conforming us into the image of Christ. And only the Lord knows what it will take to conform us into the image of His Son.

John Newton said:

> Trials are medicines which our gracious and wise physician prescribes because we need them; and he proportions the frequency and weight of them to what the case requires. Let us trust in His skill and thank Him for His prescription.[4]

I was amazed when I read a quote from Joni Eareckson Tada. What an unbelievable woman of God. As I've mentioned earlier, she is confined to a wheelchair, and she is one of the most moving speakers I have ever heard. I have had the privilege of doing some conferences with her. When I read this quote, it didn't surprise me. I experience the person of Christ in her every time I see her. She said that one of the first things she will say to God in heaven is,

> Thanks, I needed that!

Yes. God is continually after our hearts. Our hearts need to be broken by the things that break the heart of God. Without this work in us we will maneuver ourselves through life with our opinions, our judgments, and our summations. God knows that to build up our faith we need to grow continually in knowledge of Him:

> *The knowledge of the truth that leads to godliness—*
> *a faith and knowledge resting on the hope of eternal*
> *life, which God, who does not lie, promised before*
> *the beginning of time.*
>
> —TITUS 1:1–2

This will give us the certainty that He is in control. The security of knowing that His ultimate plan and destination will be accomplished in our lives.

> *Do not let your hearts be troubled. Trust in God;*
> *trust also in me.*
>
> —JOHN 14:1

God is the captain of our ship as we sail through storm-tossed seas. His Word is the lighthouse, to protect us from the hidden rocks beneath the dark waters. Ignoring the lighthouse, or "grabbing" the wheel from His capable hands, will lead to destruction. We will surely crash into the rocks and find ourselves sinking. Often we have no idea where He is taking us. I know I will often look out at the stormy sea and say,

> *I'm so glad You know where You're going, because*
> *I'm completely lost.*

We can trust His heart. We must be on a quest for His heart. That is where the peace will come in. He knows where He wants to take us. He knows what is right for us. Let's let Him get us home without a fight. And He *will* get us home. What good news.

Chapter 8
Wounded Healer

An interesting thing happened to me as I concluded the writing of this book. I've locked myself away in my office on and off for several months. I've had many people praying for God's heart to be all over these pages. It has been very important to me that this book not come across as too conceptual or clinical. I didn't want to come up with *10 Easy Answers to Why There Is Suffering*. And I most definitely did not want to come up with chapter upon chapter that "defended" God and why He chooses to allow suffering.

Pain is not an easy topic. The last thing those who are suffering need is pat answers. Tragedies, injustices, and heartaches are not easily explained away, and I'm not convinced they can or should be. What I am convinced of is that we serve a faithful God who has all the answers and is always in control. We don't necessarily need to know the reasons. We just need to know Him. We don't have to give answers to those who are suffering, but we do need to be His love to them.

This brings me to the incident that happened as I was fin-ishing this manuscript. I was intense. I was focused. I was *not* planning to be interrupted.

When my roommate, Pamela, left one morning, she told me that an exterminator was coming. Amidst my writing I had been stomping on little spiders with my feet and grab-bing them with Kleenexes as they crawled toward my desk. I was thankful that the "bug man" was coming!

Later that day, the doorbell rang. By then I had com-pletely forgotten about the exterminator's visit. I opened the door feeling frustrated because I was right in the middle of a thought. There he was. He and his bug spray were at my front door. He looked like he'd already put in a long day. He was dirty, sweaty, and thirsty. I knew it because he quickly asked me if he could have something to drink. I happily obliged, asked him if he needed anything else, and quickly ran up the stairs to get back to my computer. A couple of minutes had passed when he peeked his head in my doorway.

What do you do for a living?

Well . . . I sing . . . I speak. Ever hear of contem-porary Christian music?

Yeah. I've heard some of that.

Before I knew it he was leaning his arms over the guest chair in front of my desk telling me all about his life. I leaned back and listened as Jason told me that his wife was leaving him. He told me that he was starting to go to church. He also told me of an inoperable blood clot in a vein going to his liver. The doctors predicted it would kill him within five years. He said he had kids and couldn't get on disability. Something about having to take off six months before he could receive it. So he said he would just keep working. He couldn't afford to take the time off. At that moment I wanted to take the little vial of oil I have in my backpack and pray over him. I let him keep talking. I got up and showed him the cover art to this book.

> *This is the book I'm writing. It's called* Am I Not Still God? *and it's all about the fact that He always is. God is always with us and never without a plan. I'm so glad you are trying to put your trust in Him.*

I put two of my CDs in his hand as he kept right on talking. I was embarrassed at my own thoughts.

Hey, buddy.

I'm trying to write a book here.

I really want it to bring hope to people.

Go kill the bugs.

He shared a bit more with me and then said he had to get back to work. I told him that I wished him the best. "God bless you!" I said. He walked downstairs, and the sound of my "Christianese" farewell nauseated me. I threw a couple of "flash" prayers up for him as he walked away.

He left shortly after that, and I think I had experienced a "short" in my heart.

What were you thinking, Troccoli?

Great. Write your little book.

You want to give hope to the world, but not to Jason?

Why didn't you stop and pray over him?

I felt foolish.

About twenty minutes later the doorbell rang. *Who is it now?* I thought. *The Roto-Rooter man?* I ran downstairs, and as I opened the door with an impatient tug, I said, "Who is iiiiittttttttt? Oh. Hi!" I stopped dead in my tracks. It was Jason. He said sweetly,

I hate to bother you but I thought maybe you could give me an autograph for my daughter Faith?

Of course I can.

Hey . . . do you mind if I pray over you?

Not at all.

He bowed his head so willingly. He looked like an orphaned little boy on my front steps. It absolutely broke my heart. I put my hand over his heart and prayed for him. I knew that Jason was in the hands of God and that God would take care of His son.

We said Amen together and he thanked me as he walked to his truck. I closed the door and marveled at the Lord.

You amaze me. You know that?

How kind of You to let me have the opportunity to do what You wanted me to do the first time.

Thank You, Jesus.

I Will Exalt You, O Lord

I've been speaking and singing in different cities at my events called Evenings for Women. Powerful things happen on those nights. They've been some of the most exciting events I've done in the whole time I've had a singing career. I have performed on national television shows, I have had hit songs, and I have met a great number of celebrities. It all looks so good on paper. It all looks "successful." You now know that many of those years I was so unhappy. My heart survived with a dull ache most days. God has been so kind. He has been so loving and merciful. He has not let go of my hand. He has taught me and continues to teach me His ways. His tender hand has led me to "pleasant places." Nothing has compared to the blessing I am receiving now. I am experiencing such joy and fulfillment, speaking and singing to women from all over the world. If someone had told me years ago when I was singing in supper clubs in New York that I would be doing what I am doing now, I would definitely have thought they were in need of some psychiatric help.

For You Lifted Me Out of the Depths

Me . . . a woman who is still intimidated by a library.
Now I am an author.

Me . . . a girl who was afraid to say a word at her first church concert.
Now I am a speaker.

Me . . . the girl with a smoky lounge voice.
Now I sing for Jesus.

These are things that I get to do.
Who would have thought?

Becoming the person God longs for us to be doesn't happen easily or quickly. No one waves a magic wand over your head and—voilà!—the Proverbs 31 woman emerges. It's a process of walking each day with Him. Asking Him to penetrate your soul. Giving Him permission to mold you, change you, shake you, move you.

He has made everything beautiful in its time.
—ECCLESIASTES 3:11

Trust. What a big word. Without it we have a pretty superficial relationship with God. Every day we have a choice. Do we trust Him with the hours ahead and with whatever is around the corner? Or do we only want to "lie down in green pastures"? What we forget is, that was His original plan for us! That's why He created the Garden of Eden. He wanted us to be free of the pain that our choices, our sin, and our pride would bring upon us. We generally aren't responsible with that kind of freedom. We blur lines. We get sloppy. We are constantly tempted to "walk close to the edge." Our tendency is to "push the limits" just a little more. It's in our very nature. It's in the fiber of our being. That is why when the illuminating presence of the Holy Spirit reveals the secrets of our souls, we come under such conviction and reckon with the fact that we are in a continual battle to "restrain" ourselves.

Every day we are at the mercy of Jesus. Every day we choose to believe or not to believe. There must be some sort of foundation to build our beliefs upon in order to move forward in our faith. There must be some anchor we throw out to know we will not be moved. There has to be. Without it, every hour and every emotion that passes will toss us like the wind. That anchor must be Jesus.

It's no wonder we have a generation that has no concept of reality or of the truth of the gospel. They opt for psychics, stones, and candles because there is no cost. Nothing is required of them there. There is no bottom line to their actions or their morals without the absolute truths of God. It is very easy these days to create our own reality and adhere to it. Jesus challenges us to *His* reality. Without His influences it is easy to live for our own pleasure, to process life with a selfish heart, and to not know the meaning of the word *humility*.

Bill Gates was asked to speak before a group of high-school students. Love him or hate him, I think what he had to say to them was pretty amazing:

RULE 1:
Life is not fair. Get used to it.

RULE 2:
The world won't care about your self-esteem. The world will expect you to accomplish something before you feel good about yourself.

RULE 3:
You will not make forty thousand dollars a year right out of high school. You won't be vice president with a car phone, until you earn both.

RULE 4:
If you think your teacher is tough, wait till you get a boss. He doesn't have tenure.

RULE 5:
Flipping burgers is not beneath your dignity. Your grandparents had a word for burger flipping. They called it opportunity.

RULE 6:
If you mess up, it's not your parents' fault. Don't whine about your mistakes, but learn from them.

RULE 7:

> *Before you were born, your parents weren't as boring as they are now. They got that way from paying your bills, cleaning your clothes, and listening to you talk about how cool you are. So before you save the rain forest from the parasites of your parents' generation, try delousing the closet in your own room.*

RULE 8:

> *Your school may have done away with winners and losers, but life has not. In some schools they have abolished failing grades and they'll give you as many times as you want to get the right answer. This doesn't bear the slightest resemblance to anything in real life.*

RULE 9:

> *Life is not divided into semesters. You don't get summers and Christmas break off, and very few employers are interested in helping you find yourself. Do that on your own time.*

RULE 10:

> *Television is not real life. In real life people actually leave the coffee shop and go to jobs.*

RULE 11:

> *Be nice to nerds. Chances are you'll end up working for one.*

We are a generation of people in such desperate need of the love of God and the riches of His wisdom. That's why I yearn to be an ambassador for Jesus Christ. I pray that He will continue to use my gifts to break through the walls of lies that have been erected around the hearts of millions of unknowing people. And "truth" will never be complete unless it is viewed against *God's* truth. God is "most high." There is no one above Him. Yet we create Him in our own image. As He has pierced this heart of mine with His life, I want to be used in a way that will do the same for others. Lost sheep don't come home. They don't know how. We have to go get them. But we must remember that we can't reach others if we don't allow God to reach us.

Recently I was on a vacation with a friend and her family. We went to the beach every day and enjoyed the pool toward the end of the day. I was sitting in a lounge chair watching the kids play in the water. Little children can live in the pool until their fingers get that shriveled look. I was one of those kids. My mother would have to drag me out of the water every day in the summertime. It was the saddest part of my day. I would have been happy to grow a pair of fins.

I was enjoying the laughter of the children when I heard my friend's daughter say, "Look, Mom! Watch me!" I immediately thought about how many children make that same request. Sometimes they want the parent to watch just one time, but usually they want it to be several times. That's still me. It's just that I'm in a woman's body. Lately it happens when I step out onstage. . . .

Look, Jesus. Watch me!

I can't tell you how invigorated I am to sing and speak. There were so many seasons in my career when I dreaded getting on the airplane. I dreaded doing the concert. I dreaded the whole experience. I thought something was desperately wrong with me. "People would love to do what you're doing!" I'd often hear.

I was on the road with Amy Grant.

I toured with Michael W. Smith and Michael Bolton.

My very first record, Stubborn Love, *sold extremely well.*

I performed on The Tonight Show *and* Regis and Kathie Lee.

I opened for Jay Leno at Caesar's Palace.

My song "Everything Changes" climbed into the top five on the pop charts in 1992.

I've had many number one Christian hits.

I've won some Dove awards, and I've been nominated for Grammy awards.

I've performed with Sandi Patty, and we did a record together of songs I've always dreamed of recording.

The list goes on and on. Sounds impressive, doesn't it? I've never personally made a list of my credits before. These professional accomplishments should have resulted in "happiness," but that was not the case. I thought if I just got a certain award or sold a certain number of records then I would be fulfilled. I thought if I could just get the respect of my industry then I would be content. Maybe if I got as popular as "that artist" then I would really be successful. I would *feel* successful.

O Lord My God, I Called to You for Help

God needed to work on the very core of my soul. He needed to get me to the place where I would be content with Him. He yearned for me to be content with whatever He chose to give me. He longed for me to find joy in what He ordained for my life.

I never thought it would start happening in my forties. I never thought I would have to wait half my life before I put a toe into the land of Canaan. To catch just a glimpse of the Promised Land. All the prayers. The thousands of prayers. The tears. Through my twenties and then my thirties. But God had a plan. He always does. He needed to get me to the point in my life where when He said,

This is the way. Walk ye in it . . .

I would hear. I really would want to go. And I would find joy and peace when I got there.

And You Healed Me

When I appear at women's events, I feel like my spirit soars. I know that I am right where I need to be. I'm enjoying it with every fiber of my being. I don't want to be anywhere else, and I don't want to be anyone else.

Look, Daddy! Watch me!

I have to laugh. Some of my family members still call me aside at gatherings. . . .

You doin' all right with this gospel thing?

You makin' money?

So . . . you didn't really want to go for it like Celine Dion, huh?

It used to get to me so bad. I used to feel like a failure. Now I just smile and say, "You know, I'm really doing fine. I love what I do." What a relief.

Sing to the Lord, You His Saints

I have failed if I've missed the call of God. I want to be faithful to Him more than I want to be "successful." I want to crave His voice more than the applause of a crowd. I want to hear, "Well done, My good and faithful servant" when I see Him face to face. That is the award I seek. I want that more than any other reward this life can offer me. Jesus alone. That is my reward.

What do you seek?

What do you desire?

What are your goals?

I'm not saying that all of my motives are pure. I'm not saying that I am without sinful thoughts or actions. That is crazy. I am trapped in this body of mine like you are in yours. But I want to be His. I want to set my affections on Him. I want to be a holy woman and not just a Christian woman. I know that I don't have anything to offer anyone apart from the life of God in me.

Rejoicing Comes in the Morning

I am seeing more clearly these days. My eyesight is getting worse, but my spiritual sight is getting better. It all makes a little more sense to me now. I don't always have to "understand" to have His peace. God's peace surpasses understanding. Isn't that what it means in Philippians 4:7 when it talks about a peace that *transcends* understanding? I know that God is using the very things in my life that caused me intense suffering to bring incredible comfort. When I sing, when I speak, His healing virtue is pouring through my wounds. Whether I'm talking with the Jasons of the world, or encouraging my teenage nieces to live for Jesus, or giving an opinion at a dinner, it all is pouring from my wounds.

Death has definitely worked in me so that the life of God can work in others. And even now in the places where I am still broken, God shines His glory through my holes. He'll use us in our weakness, and we will see *His* strength. We don't have to be perfect to shine His life; we just have to live with abandonment and make ourselves available to Him. And besides, people aren't asking us to be perfect; they are asking us to be real.

When we look at the healing virtue of Jesus, we can see that it didn't come from His risen body or the empty tomb. It came from His wounds. It came at the cross. I've heard Marilyn Meberg speak on "the outlandish love of God." So many times the Lord will do things or allow things to happen to us, just to show us that He is God.

> *I will give you the treasures of darkness,*
> *riches stored in secret places,*
> *so that you may know that I am the* LORD.
> —ISAIAH 45:3

Here are lyrics that I wrote about this very thing:

> *I've known laughter, days of fun*
> *Had many hours in the sun*
> *Been to many mountains*
> *Walked along the ocean shores*
>
> *I've seen rainbows fill the sky*
> *Counted stars on summer nights*

Oh, *so many moments*
That have filled my soul with joy

But it's been the rain
It's been the storms
It's been the days when I've been worn
That I have found You, Lord
That I have seen You, Father

It's in the pain
That I have grown
Through all the sorrow I have known
But if that's what it takes for You to lead me this far
Go ahead and break my heart

I have felt the winter snow
Seen the beauty of a rose
Sat by many fires
And enjoyed the warmth of friends

I've known love and its embrace
Have felt the wind against my face
Watched the moon at midnight
Shine upon a sleeping world

But it's been the rain
It's been the storms
It's been the days that I've been worn
That I have found You, Lord
That I have seen You, Father

It's in the pain
That I have grown
Through all the sorrow I have known
But if that's what it takes for You to lead me this far
Go ahead and break my heart

I can see it on people's faces when I am onstage. They identify with the pain I speak of because it is their pain too. They know that I have been "through it." They know that the gospel is not a joke or a fairy tale to me. They find comfort in the fact that someone has felt their sorrow. They feel like if I can make it, they can make it too. I feel the same way about them. I find comfort in the testimonies I hear. They build my faith. They strengthen my courage. Many times when we see each other's wounds, we are comforted. They are a witness of the grace of God. They are a confirmation that His promises are true. We can find that very thing happening with the disciples when Jesus appeared to them after the resurrection:

> *On the evening of that first day of the week, when the disciples were together, with the doors locked for fear of the Jews, Jesus came and stood among them and said, "Peace be with you!" After he said this, he showed them his hands and side. The disciples were overjoyed when they saw the Lord.*
>
> —JOHN 20:19–20

And then we read about Thomas after the disciples exclaimed, "We have seen the Lord!"

> *But he said to them, "Unless I see the nail marks in*
> *his hands and put my finger where the nails were,*
> *and put my hand into his side, I will not believe it."*
>
> —JOHN 20:25

Watch what Jesus does:

> *A week later his disciples were in the house again,*
> *and Thomas was with them. Though the doors were*
> *locked, Jesus came and stood among them and said,*
> *"Peace be with you!" Then he said to Thomas, "Put*
> *your finger here; see my hands. Reach out your hand*
> *and put it into my side. Stop doubting and believe."*
> *Thomas said to him, "My Lord and my God!"*
>
> —JOHN 20:26–28

Through all their fear and through all their doubting, what comforted Thomas and the disciples? Jesus' wounds. In them they found joy. Their faith was renewed. They found comfort in the wounds of Jesus.

That My Heart May Sing to You and Not Be Silent

When I sing and I speak, I want people to find comfort in my wounds. I want them to encounter the Living God, the Christ. Oh, for His healing virtue to pour through our wounds!

John Newton said,

> *Preaching should break a hard heart, and heal a*
> *broken heart.*[1]

The word *compassion* comes from two Latin words that mean "to suffer with." My heart breaks when I see the tears. The Lord allows me the opportunity to share with millions of people. I am always deeply moved by their lives. I yearn to come up underneath someone's burden to help him or her bear their sorrow. I know what it feels like to be swallowed up by heartache. We shouldn't ever keep God's love to ourselves. It gives. It suffers with. It must be demonstrated.

In the last couple of years I have seen thousands of women come down to the altar for prayer. There has been no greater joy in my career than to be used in a way that would bring people healing. The women are from all walks of life. They have different backgrounds and carry different burdens. They represent different denominations and live in different places. But they all have one thing in common.

They want hope.

They want healing.

They want a touch from God.

It could be physical, emotional, or spiritual. You name it. It's there. There is nothing new under the sun. We all have the same needs.

Francis Frangipane said:

> The path toward true holiness, therefore, is a path
> full of both life and death, perils and blessings. It is a
> path upon which you will be challenged, empowered,

provoked and crucified. But you will not be disap-
pointed. If it is God you seek, it is God you will
find.[2]

At the conferences, I love that I've seen women coming
for prayer in a state of abandonment. They come expecting.
And God won't leave them empty-handed. I remember one
time singing the song I wrote called "A Baby's Prayer." I wrote
it for the shame and guilt that abortion heaps on women and
men. I wrote it also in the hopes that many babies would be
saved. At this particular women's event, the Lord moved in a
way that has completely affected how I allow Him to work
when I step out on a stage. I was in the middle of the song:

> *But if I should die*
> *Before I wake*
> *I pray her soul You'll keep*
> *Forgive her, Lord*
> *She doesn't know*
> *That You gave life to me.*

A woman who was walking down the center aisle of the
church caught my eye. I just thought she was returning from
the rest room. She didn't ever sit down but walked right past
the pews and climbed the first couple of steps toward the
altar. She then fell to her knees. Her head was right next to
my left knee, and I stroked her hair as I continued singing. I
prayed that God would give me *His* prayers for her when I got
through with the song. Before I knew it her humble action
caused an avalanche of women to descend upon the front of

the church. I prayed. The weeping was loud. The forgiving hand of God was soft and gentle.

I've prayed for the Lord to touch . . .

Marriages, separations, and divorces

Disease

Depression

Relationships, bitterness, and adultery

Sexual addictions

Eating disorders

Financial stress

Compulsions

Abuse

Decisions

Hopelessness

Self-esteem

"Sin-sickness" (sometimes sin has its own punishment)

The list is long. We lose our way. We want hope. We want forgiveness. We want restoration. We want freedom. The enemy wants to kill our faith. He wants us to question God. He yearns for us to mock God and rebel against Him. First he kills our faith, and then he slowly tries to kill us. I heard someone say that Satan takes a dagger toward us to destroy us. But the nail-pierced hand of Jesus turns it into a scalpel to form us more into the image of Christ. Never forget that what the devil intends for harm God will use for good.

You Removed My Sackcloth and Clothed Me with Joy

We must continually take trips to the cross. We must live a life of repentance. We must keep our hands open so that God can fill them. He will forgive. He will restore. He will set free. We can be different from what life "sets us up to be."

Hebrews 10:22 says:

> *Let us draw near to God with a sincere heart in full*
> *assurance of faith, having our hearts sprinkled to*
> *cleanse us from a guilty conscience and having our*
> *bodies washed with pure water.*

God's worthiness flows into our unworthiness and we become worthy. If we want the Lord to empower us we must come under His rule. His commands are for us and not against us. They are not to constrain us but to free us. Beth Moore says:

*The don'ts God has given us, free us to accomplish
the do's.*[3]

We must not miss the life God has for us. A life marked by
His blessings. A life marked with supernatural provision. A
life that is lived by divine leading.

This is one of my favorite psalms:

I will exalt you, O LORD,
   for you lifted me out of the depths
   and did not let my enemies gloat over me.
O LORD my God, I called to you for help
   and you healed me.
O LORD, you brought me up from the grave;
   you spared me from going down into the pit.

Sing to the LORD, you saints of his;
   praise his holy name.
For his anger lasts only a moment,
   but his favor lasts a lifetime;
weeping may remain for a night,
   but rejoicing comes in the morning. . . .

You turned my wailing into dancing;
   you removed my sackcloth and clothed me with joy,
that my heart may sing to you and not be silent.
   O LORD my God, I will give you thanks forever.
      —PSALM 30:1–5, 11–12

So there will be the storms. It will get treacherous and dark. It will feel like a never-ending night.

But the morning will come.

The sun will rise again.

It will be a new day.

You will possess a new hope.

And you will see and receive new mercies.

Jesus Christ is not a security from storms. He is *perfect* security in storms.

Yes . . . He is still God.

Epilogue
The Mourning After

We were in the final stages of editing this book. I was reading through these pages for the tenth time when something happened that rocked the whole world. On September 11, 2001, America was attacked, carving a wound so deep that history will always bear the scar. I found it strange yet comforting that I had bathed myself in the hope of God in preparation for writing this manuscript. What timing. I am so thankful. In the hours that followed the shocking attack, I needed to read my own words.

Now, all I can do is sit at my desk and write the passion of my heart. I must proclaim it. It's what I know to be true.

In the words of Charles Spurgeon quoted earlier:

As sure as ever God puts His children in the furnace He will be in the furnace with them.

And as Watchman Nee said:

To hold on to the plough, while wiping our tears—
this is Christianity.

The last couple of days I have been in somewhat of a fog.
I certainly have been grieving. I know that many of you have
as well. My beloved New York has lost so many souls, and the
drastically altered majestic skyline is a reminder of the presence of evil in this world.

All I could do as I watched the horror of September 11
was cry out to Jesus. I begged for His mercy and I pleaded His
blood upon this nation as the blood of thousands was shed
because of the horrific terrorist acts.

As the fire and smoke were filling the skies over New
York and Washington, D.C., I pictured what was filling the
skies in the heavenlies. A war was going on. As I watched the
news I realized that just as America wasn't sure who its
enemy was, many in America are blind to the enemy of their
souls: the one who comes to kill, steal, and destroy—not just
physically, but definitely spiritually as well. That is an even
sadder state of affairs.

As I write with teary eyes, I am reminded of these simple
but profound truths:

God is in control.

God will ultimately have His way.

Let us keep an attitude of prayer, knowing that that is
where the true battle is won. We gain wisdom on our knees
. . . power is released on our knees . . . love pours into our
hearts on our knees.

May we as Christians humble ourselves under His mighty hand so that the whole world will benefit from how we conduct ourselves during this terrible time. We do have a divine confidence, and we can trust Him beyond our human reasoning.

King David said:

> *Why are you downcast, O my soul?*
> —Psalm 43

Worship Him today. Let us talk to our souls—sing to our souls—reminding ourselves of the reason we put our hope in Jesus Christ.

We may not understand our circumstances, but we can understand the character of God:

> *He is a God of justice, of compassion, of love and mercy.*

> *He is holy and righteous.*

> *He is all-powerful, all-knowing . . . ever present.*

We are in a time of extreme darkness right now. But remember, darkness isn't dark to God. He sees perfectly.

Be assured that God Almighty has roused Himself from His throne. . . .

> *Disease will not have the last say.*

> *Death will not have the last say.*

Immorality will not have the last say.

Our questions will not have the last say.

Terrorists will not have the last say.

Destruction will not have the last say.

Evil, certainly, will not have the last say.

Our God—our Jehovah, our King of kings and Lord of lords—will most definitely have the last say.

We will be eternally with Him one day. His promises will all be fulfilled. We will be certain of the fact that He never left us or forgot us.

Good will triumph over evil.

> *Every knee will bow, and every tongue will confess that Jesus Christ is Lord.*
>
> —SEE ROMANS 14:11

Count on it.

Notes

Chapter 1: Am I Not Still God?

1. Corrie ten Boom, as quoted in *Heroes of the Faith* (Uhrichsville, Ohio: Barbour, n.d.), 75.

Chapter 2: Where Are You?

1. Oswald Chambers, *My Utmost for His Highest* (Grand Rapids: Discovery House, 1935), May 9.

Chapter 3: Brace Yourself

1. Mike Mason, *The Gospel According to Job* (Wheaton, Ill.: Crossway Books, 1994), 132.
2. Ibid., 153.
3. Philip D. Yancey, *The Bible Jesus Read* (Grand Rapids: Zondervan, 1999), 52.

4. Martha Bolton, *Never Ask Delilah for a Trim . . . and Other Good Advice*. Copyright ©1998 by Martha Bolton. Published by Servant Publications, P. O. Box 8617, Ann Arbor, MI 48107. Used with permission.

Chapter 5: Never without Hope

1. Charles Spurgeon, as quoted in *Heroes*, 6.
2. Dwight L. Moody, as quoted in *Heroes*, 88.
3. As quoted in Raymond McHenry, *Something to Think About* (Peabody, Mass.: Hendrickson, 1998), 130.

Chapter 6: Complete Trust

1. *Houston Post*, April 19, 1992, sec. A-27, as quoted in *Something to Think About*.
2. Mother Teresa, as quoted in *Something to Think About*, 202.

Chapter 7: Winds of Faith

1. Watchman Nee, as quoted in *Heroes*, 136.
2. C. S. Lewis, as quoted in *Heroes*, 106.
3. Martin Luther, as quoted in *Heroes*, 139.
4. John Newton, as quoted in *Heroes*, 12.

Chapter 8: Wounded Healer

1. John Newton, as quoted in *Heroes*, 37.

2. Francis Frangipane, *Holiness, Truth and the Presence of God* (Marion, Iowa: Advancing Church Publications, 1986, revised 1989), introduction.
3. Beth Moore, speaking engagement.

Sources for Songs

"A Baby's Prayer" (page 196)

Lyrics by Kathy Troccoli. Copyright © 1996 Sony/ATV Songs LLC and New Spring Publishing Inc. All rights on behalf of Sony/ATV Songs LLC administered by Sony/ATV Music Publishing, 8 Music Square West, Nashville, TN 37203. All rights reserved. Used by permission.

"Break My Heart" (page 192)

Lyrics by Kathy Troccoli. Copyright © 2000 Sony/ATV Songs LLC, Bird Wins Publishing and Hits R Us Music. All rights on behalf of Sony/ATV Songs LLC administered by Sony/ATV Music Publishing, 8 Music Square West, Nashville, TN 37203. All rights reserved. Used by permission.

"Goodbye for Now" (page 127)
Lyrics by Kathy Troccoli. Copyright © 1998 Sony/ATV Songs LLC and New Spring Publishing Inc. All rights on behalf of Sony/ATV Songs LLC administered by Sony/ATV Music Publishing, 8 Music Square West, Nashville, TN 37203. All rights reserved. Used by permission.

"How Would I Know" (page 168)
Lyrics by Jackie Gouché-Ferris. Copyright © 1997 JAAC Publishing (BMI).

"Love Was Never Meant to Die" (page 148)
Lyrics by Kathy Troccoli. Copyright © 1991 Emily Boothe, Inc. (BMI)/BMG Music Publishing, 14000 18th Avenue South, Nashville, TN 37212. All rights reserved. Used by permission.

"When I Look at You" (page 141)
Lyrics by Kathy Troccoli. Copyright © 1998 Sony/ATV Songs LLC and Different Road Music. All rights on behalf of Sony/ATV Songs LLC administered by Sony/ATV Music Publishing, 8 Music Square West, Nashville, TN 37203. All rights reserved. Used by permission.

Also Available from Kathy Troccoli

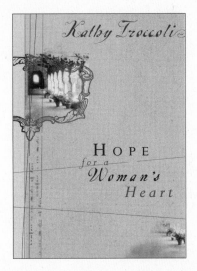

HOPE FOR A WOMAN'S HEART

Award-winning Christian artist, Kathy Troccoli has also gained popularity as a speaker and respected author in recent years. Known for her deep compassion and strong convictions, Kathy ministers hope to hurting women in her book, *Hope for a Woman's Heart*. Having gone through difficult times in her own life—including losing both of her parents to cancer and struggling with depression—she speaks with the conviction of one who has walked the road of the brokenhearted. Through song lyrics, real-life stories, and inspirational thoughts, Kathy praises God for His sovereignty and encourages women to lean on the One who can offer rest, comfort, and healing.